AN ADVANCED LATIN SYNTAX

AN ADVANCED LATIN SYNTAX

BY

A. L. FRANCIS, M.A.,

Sometime Fellow of Jesus College, Cambridge, and late Head Master of Blundell's School, Tiverton,

AND

H. F. TATUM, M.A.,

Sometime Scholar of Balliol College, Oxford, and Ireland University Scholar, late Assistant Master of Blundell's School, Tiverton.

CAMBRIDGE
AT THE UNIVERSITY PRESS
1919

CAMBRIDGE
UNIVERSITY PRESS

University Printing House, Cambridge CB2 8BS, United Kingdom

Cambridge University Press is part of the University of Cambridge.

It furthers the University's mission by disseminating knowledge in the pursuit of education, learning and research at the highest international levels of excellence.

www.cambridge.org
Information on this title: www.cambridge.org/9781316611968

First published 1919
First paperback edition 2016

A catalogue record for this publication is available from the British Library

ISBN 978-1-316-61196-8 Paperback

PREFACE

THIS work is an attempt to deal in a short compass with late and exceptional idioms of Latin, and to bring them into harmony with the principles of the language. It is based on Roby and Riemann, and we owe some debt to the notes in Papillon's Virgil, Duff's Juvenal and other editions: but the whole of the plan and conclusions, as well as a considerable part of the argument and materials, are our own.

A. L. F.
H. F. T.

TIVERTON,
October 11, 1919.

CONTENTS

(Further details are given in the Index of Subjects.)

SUBSTANTIVES

NUMBER, SUBJECT AND PREDICATE

1. Plural of Class. The plural may stand for a type, where we should use the singular with the indefinite article: **Regulum et Scauros** *a Regulus, a Scaurus* Hor. *Od.* i 12 37: **Ismara** *an Ismarus* Virg. *Ec.* 2 37: **hoc nocuit Lamiarum caede madenti** of one Lamia only Juv. iv 154: **Delphinum caudas utero commissa luporum** of Scylla Virg. *Aen.* iii 428. Sometimes it implies contempt also: **Mamercorum alapas** Juv. viii 192: **planipedes Fabios** *ib.* referring to individual types: **nec tu mensarum morsus horresce** *such a thing as eating tables* Virg. *Aen.* iii 394. To this may perhaps be traced the **frequent** use of plural for singular with **Class-nouns** in poetry: **vitreo daturus nomina ponto** *a name* Hor. *Od.* iv 2 4: esp. **nives, aestates** etc., *snow* and *summer in general.* See **62** and **79** for Class in singular (*a sun, the good man* etc.).

2. Predication. A predicate may relate to the Subject or Object of a sentence (as with verbs of making etc.), or to the indirect object: as, **quibus bellum volentibus erat** Tac. *Agr.* 18: **nomen Trinummo fecit** Plaut. *Trin.* 20 (**Trinummo** predicate of **libro** understood): **nomen histrionibus inditum** Liv. vii 2 6: **licet esse beatis** Hor. *Sat.* i 1 19; or together with its subject may form the abl. absolute or other substantival expressions as **ademptus Hector** Hor. *Od.* ii 4 10: **subeunda dimicatio** Liv. ii 13 2 (**sec. 174**).

3. Several subjects combined take a predicate in the plural. If of different genders, the plural masculine is used of persons, neuter of things. Two different persons take a plural predicate even in disjunctive use: as, **neque ego neque tu id fecimus** Ter. *Ad.* i 2 23, like the colloquial English *neither you nor I were there*: **tu aut ille possitis** Servilius in Cic. *Fam.* iv 55:

except sometimes when the subjects form one idea, as, **tempus necessitasque, senatus populusque,** or when each subject marks a separate fact, as **intercessit C. Caelius, C. Pansa, tribuni plebis** Cael. ap. Cic. *Fam.* viii 8: **consules...Fulvius in agrum Cumanum, Claudius in Lucanos abiit** Liv. xxv 19 6: **Orgetorigis filia atque unus ex filiis captus est** Caes. *b. g.* i 26. Or subordinate terms may be neglected: **tu tuaque omnia curae sunt** Cic. *Fam.* vi 3: **ipse meique...vescor** Hor. *S.* ii 6 65: **amor tuus ac iudicium...utrum plus dignitatis sit allaturus** Cic. *Fam.* x 24 1: **ego populusque Romanus bellum indico** Liv. i 32 14.

Two singulars with **cum** may take a plural verb: **Sulla cum Scipione ...conditiones contulerunt** (with words between) Cic. *Ph.* xii 11 27.

Absente and **praesente** are found in inscriptions with plural subject (*Schema Pindaricum*): so humorously **absente nobis** for **me** Ter. *Eun.* iv 3 7.

The adverbs **benè, pulcrè** (Cic.), **frustrà** (Liv.) etc. may be predicated with **esse.**

4. Of several subjects in apposition the verb agrees with the nearest: as, **Corioli oppidum captum est: Corinthum** (fem.) **totius Graeciae lumen exstinctum** Cic. *de Imp.* v 11: even **Quis nisi latrones putant** *Ph.* iv 4 9. Unless sense forbids, as, **Hannibal peto pacem** Liv. xxx 30 29: **Tullia, deliciolae nostrae, munusculum tuum flagitat** Cic. *Att.* i 8.

5. A pronominal subject agrees with an **identical predicate** (denoting the significance of a thing, fact or name). **Ea erat confessio caput rerum Romam esse** Liv. i 45 5: **Alesiam, quod est oppidum Mandubiorum** Caes. *b. g.* vii 68 1: **Pompeio, quod imperii R. lumen fuit** Cic. *Ph.* ii 22 54: **animum dico, mentem quam saepe vocamus** Lucr. iii 9: **(consulatus) eam esse aram libertatis, id columen** Liv. vi 37 4: **alterius exercitus quod subsidium esset** (*to be*) vii 23 4: **gladiatores quod erat spectaculum** ix 40 17: **id munimentum fortuna urbis habuit** (meaning Horatius) ii 10 2: **hoc opus, hic labor est** Virg. *Aen.* vi 129 (*the* task). But this use cannot extend to a predicate of fact. **Nec sopor illud erat** (*a sleep*) Virg. *Aen.* iii 173: **si hoc profectio et non fuga est** Liv. ii 38 5: **ut quod segnitia erat sapientia appellaretur** Tac. *Hist.* i 49: **Indus, qui est omnium fluminum maximus** Cic. *N. D.* ii 52 130.

A pronoun may define words beyond its strict agreement: as in **hic terror** (= **huius rei terror**) **omnes convertit** Liv. x 13 5: **quo numine laeso** *by what insult to her majesty* Virg. *Aen.* i 8; **ex eo numero qui fuerunt** Cic. *de lege agr.* ii 14 37. (**Adverbial Adj.**, **sec. 81–2.**)

6. Collective nouns (**pars, multitudo etc.**) take a verb in the plural in Livy: as, **Cetera classis fugerunt** with intervening words xxxv 26 9: but not in Cicero except the word **partim.** (There is the same difference in regard to **quisque,** which in Livy stands in apposition to a plural subject: as, **suas quisque abirent domos** Liv. ii 7 1: **pictores et poetae suum quisque opus considerari vult** Cic. *Off.* i 41 147: see **sec. 96.**)

7. A copula expressing identity or definition will (on account of its position) agree with the predicated noun: **non omnis error stultitia dicenda est** Cic. *de Div.* ii 43 90: **amantium irae amoris integratio est** Ter. *And.* iii 3 23: **vexillum clxxxvi homines erant** Liv. viii 8 8: **omnia vel medium fiat mare** Virg. *Ec.* 8 58: **not** with a **general** or **Class-predicate: captivi militum praeda fuerant** Liv. xxi 15 1: **quae velut claustra** (indefinite article) **Etruriae erat** ix 32 11. Ambiguity may be avoided by using the predicative dative as in **impedimento fuit**; or otherwise: **in pueris esse, senex e puero factus, pro cauto timidus appellatus 35** (*b*).

8. Apposition is the attributive use of a noun. Besides its qualifying or defining sense, as in **victor exercitus, Q. Fabius pictor, instar montis equum,** it often affects the whole sentence adverbially in such phrases as **victor rediit, sciebat homo sapiens** *he knew in his wisdom* (Gk. σοφὸς ὢν). **Vir, homo** are very commonly so used (see under **Adjective, Adverbial use**). A proper name may qualify a common noun, as, **corrector Bestius** Hor. *Ep.* i 15 37.

Apposition of part and whole is perhaps imitated from Homer in **Latagum occupat os** Virg. *Aen.* x 698, but see **sec. 1–6.**

9. Instances of a **Greek construction** are **Sensit medios delapsus in hostes** Virg. *Aen.* ii 377 and (perhaps) **Uxor invicti Iovis esse nescis** Hor. *Od.* iii 27 73, where the main subject keeps its case through dependent clauses. **Rettulit Aiax Esse Iovis pronepos** Ov. *Met.* xiii 141: **orantes primi transmittere** Virg. *Aen.* vi 313: **Id silentio noctis conati non magnâ iacturâ sese effecturos sperabant** Caes. *b.g.* vii 26 1 (= **conatos**). (Cat. has **ait fuisse** iv 1 and Tac. **dissentire manifestus** *Ann.* ii 57.) Livy follows this practice even in abl. absolute and gerundive clauses: **cogendo ipse agmen locum praebet** xxxix 49 3: **gerendo solus censuram** ix 29 8: and **contione adveniens habitâ** xli 10 13: **id consules, ambos ad exercitum morando, quaesisse** xxii 34 10. Tacitus has **Suam ipsi vitam narrare fiduciam arbitrati sunt** *Agr.* 1. A Grecism parallel to the above appears in **Cetera quâ iaceant...ruinâ ante oculos sunt** (δηλοῖ ὄντα) *Aen.* xi 310.

10. Nominative and Vocative. The imperative has no subject except in archaic Latin: **agedum pontifex publicus...praei verba** Liv. viii 9 4: **audi tu populus Albanus** i 24 9: but it may have a nominative predication for the vocative: *e.g.* **proice tela manu, sanguis meus** *you who are my kin* Virg. *Aen.* vi 835, but **mi anime** if one with the person addressed. A vocative may itself have a nominative predicate, as **primus appellate** Plin. *H.N.* vii 117, but there are many instances of a vocative predicate: **credite amice** Cat. lxxvii 1: **macte esto** *be magnified*: **miserande iaceres** Virg. *Aen.* x 327: **tune etiam spoliis indute meorum Eripiare mihi?** xii 948: **quibus Hector ab oris Exspectate venis?** ii 283: **heu terrâ ignotâ canibus date praeda Latinis Alitibusque iaces** ix 485. In the following the vocative is perhaps a sort of quotation: **Matutine pater seu Iane libentius audis** Hor. *S.* ii 6 20 like Milton's *Or hear'st thou rather pure ethereal stream* [*P. L.* iii 7].

ACCUSATIVE CASE

11. The **Accusative case** is the external or internal extension of the Verb. Transitive Verbs use the former.

Intransitive Verbs may become transitive when compounded with **prepositions** of motion or position as **adire, adiacere** (rarely), **intercinere**, and in good prose **antecedo** and **praecedo**, but only in a literal sense. **Anteeo** and **praeeo** however take the dative literally, while **praeeo** means *to dictate* with the accusative, and **anteiri** *to be surpassed*. **Anteeo** is also transitive.

Compounds with e and ex forming a single idea may become transitive: as, **Evadere pestem, egredi relationem, praeturam, urbem**: **exire vim, ictus** Virg.: **excedere urbem** or **modum**.

12. Two Accusatives may follow a transitive compound verb in a local sense: as, **transmittere flumen equites**: **arbitrum illum adegit** Cic. *Off.* iii 16: similarly **iusiurandum** Caes. *b. c.* ii 18 5: Livy uses **iureiurando** (ii 1 6) as though with **adstringo.** Sometimes the new accusative displaces the old, as **Socios circumtulit undâ** Virg. *Aen.* vi 229: **circumdat oppidum vallo** as well as **oppido** (dat.) **vallum**.

13. Verbs of Making, Calling, Thinking include **ducere, numerare** *to account*, **reddere** *to make*. Most of them are used in the passive as copulas, including **duco** and **numero** but not **reddo**.

14. Asking, Teaching and Concealing. These seldom take two accusatives or an accusative in the passive. **Rogo** *request* has either accusative separately, but both only in **rogo populum tribunos**, or in poetry as **Otium divos rogat** Hor. *Od.* ii 16 1. **Flagito** rarely has both accusatives as in Caes. *b. g.* i 16 1 **quotidie Caesar Aeduos frumentum flagitare**, and in Hor. **Nec potentem amicum Largiora flagito** *Od.* ii 18 12. Otherwise **ab** is used or the genitive, as **Consulis auxilium flagitare**. **Oro** takes no second accusative except such words as **illud** and **multa**: **hoc te vehementer oro** etc. Besides **Rogo** in questions, **te id consulo** Cic. *Att.* vii 20.

Asking favours rarely if ever takes acc. in the passive. Pliny has **pretium reposceris** *Ep.* vii 12: **exigor praetorium** Caecilius in Gellius xv 14. **Rogor** of the person without acc. is common.

Doceo has the double acc. regularly but none in the passive except in Hor.: **Motus doceri gaudet Ionicos** *Od.* iii 6 21 and **Docte sermones utriusque linguae** iii 8 5.

Celo with two accusatives is colloquial: **Te celavi sermonem** Cic. *ad Fam.* ii 16. **Celare aliquem** is regular with or without **de re. Te de rebus celatum** v 2 7. **Vereor ne celatum me illis ipsis non honestum sit** *Ph.* ii 13 32: also of course **celare rem.**

15. Intransitive Verbs denoting State may take an External Accusative. To **doleo** and **horreo** may be added **palleo, indignor, sitio, depereo,** besides use in Com.

16. Passive (or middle) participles often take an accusative of anything affecting the *surface of an object* as dress or other appendage. These *external* accusatives may be accounted for in some cases by a lost middle voice. **Exuitur cornua** is the passive (or middle) of **exuere cornua alicui (exuit hic humero pharetram** Ov. *Met.* ii 419), the dative of the active becoming the subject. But **Unum exuta pedem vinclis** *Aen.* iv 518, is like the accusatives of respect. Various relations are expressed: **inscripti nomina regum** Virg. *Ecl.* 4 106: **inductae varias plumas** Hor. *A.P.* 2: **laevo suspensi loculos tabulamque lacerto** *Ep.* i 1 56: **perque pedes traiectus lora tumentes** Virg. *Aen.* ii 273 and **Delphinum caudas utero commissa luporum** iii 428: **nodoque sinus collecta fluentes** i 320: **vellera Tyrios incocta rubores** *Geo.* iii 307: **Sidoniam picto chlamydem circumdata limbo** *Aen.* iv 137. It is of course entirely different from the Accusative of Respect, which is internal. **Decipitur laborem** accepted in Hor. *Od.* ii 13 38 for *laborum* is difficult to parallel.

17. Accusative of Motion may be external as well as internal. The former includes the use with prepositions and the accusative of names of towns (**filiam Romam nuptum dederat**

for both external and internal). **Ad** with towns signifies *to the neighbourhood.* With adjectives thus: **Capuam, urbem florentissimam,** or **Tarquinios, in urbem florentissimam**: or **Lacedaemonium Tarentum** Hor. *Od.* iii 5 56. Provinces and countries take **in** not **ad**: Crete, Cyprus, Rhodus, Bosporus are sometimes dealt with as towns, and we find also **ad Cretam.** In poetry **Italiam venit** Virg. *Aen.* i 6.

18. Cognate Accusative: (Apposition to idea of Verb). This is never a mere repetition of the Verb but a new aspect of it: **vox hominem sonat** Virg. *Aen.* i 328 = **hominis vocem** or **sonum**: **Cyclopa moveri** *to dance the 'Cyclops' dance* Hor. *Ep.* ii 2 125: **hoc vincite** Virg. *Aen.* v 196: **census es mancipia** *you were registered under 'slaves owned'* Cic. *pro Flacc.* 32 80: **intercessisse pro eis magnam pecuniam** *Att.* vi 1 5. With **stillo, resono, oleo** also the accusative is cognate: **litora alcyonem resonant** Virg. *Geo.* iii 338: **verbera insonuit** *Aen.* vii 451: **spem fronte serenat** iv 477. Passive **Dormitur hiems** Mart. xiii 59. After noun: **secus, sec. 21.**

French has no cognate accusative: *dormir d'un profond sommeil* to rest in deep slumber.

19. This accusative is used in various ways to express motion, space, time and age.

Motion (Internal, signifying nature of motion not place which is External): **exsequias ire** *go to a funeral*: **pessum ire** *go to ground*: **infitias ire** *go denying*: to this belong the supine in **-um,** and **venum** with **do** and **eo.**

Space traversed: **tria milia repimus** Hor. *S.* i 5 25: **maria omnia vecti** Virg. *Aen.* i 524: **terras omnes ferimur** v 627: in the passive **unda natatur** Ov. *Tr.* v 2 25: or **measured** (also in ablative): **ducenos pedes alti**: **quinque milia** or **milibus abest.**

Time Extended: **flet noctem**: **diem ex die exspectare**: often with **per**: or **time measured**: **abhinc biennium** (or **biennio**): **ante diem tertium** with **die tertio ante**: hence to denote

Age: **novem annos natus**: also by genitive of quality: comparative age under ablative of comparison.

20. Adverbial Accusative. **Vicem** *extent, part, likeness*: **magnam vicem** *to a great extent*: **nostram vicem irasci** *on my behalf*: **pecudum vicem obtruncari** *like sheep*: **humanam vicem** with **convertere** Hor. *Epod.* v 88 is perhaps cognate meaning *change with a human change.*

To the adverbial accusatives from adjectives may be added **Immane quantum discrepat** Hor. *Od.* i 27 6, an imitation of Greek (*it differs vastly*; an immense how much): **perfidum ridens, aeternum vale, tertium consul, uno aut summum altero.** Hor. has **multum celer** *S.* ii 3 147, **dulce ridentem** *Od.* i 22 24: Virgil **longum vale** *Ec.* 3 79, **intonuit laevum** *Aen.* ix 631, **multum** and **tantum fluere** *Geo.* ii 100, **miserabile victis hostibus insultans** *Aen.* xii 338, the accusative probably with **insultans,** as it is not a mere adverb but must express directly some aspect of the verb. This accusative often expresses an effect on the senses: **magnum loqui** (**dulce loquentem** Hor. *Od.* i 22 24 is more normal than **ridentem** above); **grave olens** (but **bene olere**); **suave rubens**; **pingue quoddam sonantibus** Cic. *pro Arch.* 10 26. The neuter plural is used in **insanire sollennia**: **omnia Mercurio similis** (with an adjective, comp. **multum confusus**): **insueta rudentem** Virg. *Aen.* viii 248; to be distinguished from external accusative with **palleo, doleo**: the following *e.g.* are adverbial: **multa gemens, multa dolens, transversa fremunt** *Aen.* v 19.

These neuters are strictly nouns, abstract and indeclinable, like **satis, nihil** (**nihil miseriti sunt** Liv. v 45 4), **parum, plus, adfatim, partim, abunde,** and are used in the nominative and accusative only.

21. Accusative with Nouns. **Qui reditus Romam** Cic. *Phil.* ii 42 108: **iusta sum orator datus** Plaut. *Amph.* 34: **quid tibi istanc tactio est** *Poen.* 1308: **poenas timendumst** Lucr. i 111. The infinitive and supine in **-um** govern cases like the Finite Verb.

Virile and **muliebre secus** are used as cognate accusatives after nouns in Livy and Tacitus: **liberorum capitum virile secus ad decem milia capta** Liv. xxvi 47 1 and in Tac. *Hist.* v 13: **id genus** etc. Cic.

22. Accusative or Nominative **in Apposition** to the sentence. The following are in the accusative: **initium armorum** Tac. *Ann.* i 27: **causas bello** ii 64: **in posterum ultionem** *Hist.* i 44: **tormenti genus** Virg. *Aen.* viii 487: **solatia luctus** xi 62: **iaculum mittit Principium pugnae** ix 53: **omen pugnae** x 311: **Triste ministerium** vi 223: **quod..regnum exercerent** Liv. v 2 8. This would be the Internal Completion of the predicate and therefore express the character and intention of the act. A developement of **18.**

The following in apposition to a passive or impersonal sentence may be considered nominative. **Maiestatis crimina subdebantur, vinclum et necessitas silendi** Tac. *Ann.* iii 67, where **vinclum** is perhaps in apposition to **crimina**: but elsewhere there is no such alternative: as, **magna, id quod necesse erat accidere, perturbatio facta est** Caes. *b. g.* iv 29 3: so **mirabile dictu**: **satis una superque vidimus exscidia** Virg. *Aen.* ii 641 = **satis est quod vidimus**, for **satis** is never in agreement. So **adlapsa sagitta est Incertum qua pulsa manu** *Aen.* xii 320. Both are akin to the cognate or adverbial accusative.

Accusative of Respect. This is rare in prose and with Active Verbs. **Saepes apibus florem depasta salicti** Virg. *Ec.* 1 54: **ardentes oculos suffusi sanguine** *Aen.* ii 210: **perculsae corda** Lucr. i 13: **formam adsimulata Camerti** *Aen.* xii 224: **ad surgentem conversi lumina solem** xii 172 though perhaps middle is not transitive as in the participles of 'dress' above.

DATIVE CASE

23. Without attempting to classify all the datives it may be remarked that 'to' and 'for' mainly denote a difference in the governing word, and both might be included under '**External Direction.**' Another dative often called **Predicative** might be added of '**Internal Direction**' (sec. **33**) denoting identity with an abstract idea.

24. With adjectives. Tacitus prefers **in** with the accusative: **aetate et formâ non dissimili in dominum** *Ann.* ii 39:

Livia gravis in rempublicam mater i 10: compare **Mare omne in austrum cessit** ii 23. Livy has **gratior in vulgus** ix 33 5. Of special adjectives **aemulus** governs the genitive but the dative sometimes in poetry: **alienus** with the dative means *foreign* or of things *unsuited* or *opposed*: with gen. or abl. *inconsistent.* The preposition **ab** is also used with the last meaning, and with the first in comedy. **Par** is found with abl. of comparison in Ovid *Fast.* vi 804. With **similis** gen. is the more usual. **Superstes** either gen. or dat. in Cic. Add with dat. **natus, paratus**: **amicus dispar** gen. or dat.

25. With compound verbs the prepositions in their literal sense tend to preserve their constructions: but **subeo succedo** have both dative and accusative in the sense of approaching: **adequitant vallo** Liv. ix 22 4. Generally the dative expresses tendency not motion: as with **adicio adimo supersum antecello praesto** *excel* (acc. rarely) **posthabeo intercedo** (*oppose*) **excello** (rare) **subvenio interdico** (abl. of thing forbidden) **confero. Impono** *to place on* not *in.* Cic has Prep. with **coniungo, discrepo, disto.**

The preposition is often omitted in poetry: **figat humo** for **affigat: ventura desuper urbi** *Aen.* ii 47: **pedibus talaria nectit** iv 239: **iaculatus puppibus ignes** ii 276: **rideo** for **arrideo** Hor. *Od.* ii 6 14.

26. 'Possessive' dative. Properly with **esse** with the meaning '*I have,*' it is used by Virgil with many other verbs with the implied sense of belonging, as in the French *il lui a cassé la tête.* **Pallas huic filius una......tura dabant** Virg. *Aen.* viii 104: **Turno fiducia cessit** x 276: **mansit sententia Turno. Olli dura quies oculos et ferreus urget Somnus** x 745: **Ardet apex capiti** x 270: **huic gladio** (abl.) **latus haurit apertum** x 314: **verba Quae tuto tibi magna volant** xi 381: **cuius amor mihi crescit in horas** *Ec.* 10 73: **tauris iuga solvet** 4 41.

Also in prose with parts of the body. **Sese omnes ad pedes Caesari proiecerunt** Caes. *b. g.* i 31 2: **puero caput arsisse ferunt** Liv. i 39: **cornici oculum (percussit)** proverb in Cic. *Flacc.* 20 46. And in other connections: as, **militanti in Hispaniâ pater moritur** Liv.

xxix 29 6. There would be many crosses between this and others following, and indeed the distinction is mainly one of convenience.

27. Dative of the Agent. This really signifies the person for whom an act exists whether as a duty or an achievement: hence it is rarer of completed action. **Multis ille bonis flebilis occidit: nulli flebilior quam tibi, Vergili** Hor. *Od.* i 24 9: **facilis partienti** Liv. ix 19 8. With the gerundive the ablative with **ab** may always be used when required for clearness or emphasis, but this is almost confined to Cicero. The dative is used with the ordinary gerund in Liv. vi 35 7 **ad sciscendum plebi** *for the people to vote*: and the ablative with **ab** with the gerundive in the sense of gerund Liv. ix 40 17 **inde initium fori ornandi ab ædilibus.**

Instances of use with past time are the semi-adjectival **conspectus**; **auditus** Liv. v 38 6: **neglecta patribus** viii 20 2: **scripta sunt plura nemini** Cic. *Fin.* i 4 11: in poetry it is common with any part of the passive; **lapides Pyrrhae iactos** Virg. *Ec.* 6 51: **carmina quae scribuntur aquae potoribus** Hor. *Ep.* i 19 3. **Legionem Fausto conscriptam** Cic. *Att.* viii 3 7 has the original sense *for Faustus.*

28. Dative of Direction of Motion (Dative of the Goal). Some familiar instances may be locatives. It is almost entirely poetical but is not a Grecism. **Toto proiectus corpore terrae** *Aen.* xi 87: **spolia coniciunt igni** xi 194: **terrae defigitur arbos** *Geo.* ii 290: **nec fraus te perferet Auno** *Aen.* xi 717: **caelo educere certant** ii 553: **quos mitteret umbris Inferias** xi 81: **aversos sternere morti** xii 464: **molli compellere hibisco** *Ec.* 2 30: **viam adfectat Olympo** *Geo.* iv 562: **demisere neci** *Aen.* ii 85: **linquere terrae** v 795: **reliquit arenae** xii 382: **fusum labris** 417: **tumulo mittunt** vi 380: **Cocyto eructat arenam** 297. Horace has **ponto Unda recumbit** *Od.* i 12 32, and Tacitus **ruptores pacis ultioni et gloriae mactandos** *Ann.* ii 13: **incessit itineri et proelio** i 51. The purpose is not of the subject but of the act, *in marching and battle array.* Add **destino** not in Cic.

29. Dative of Advantage.

The direction is either to a person or to a thing. Add to the common instances **timeo, metuo, consulo, caveo** with dative of the person concerned. The object may be a person under a metaphor or metonym, as **caro oneri timet** Virg. *Aen.* xi 550, *he trembles for his precious burden*: **aurea condet Saecula qui rursus Latio** vi 193: or a thing personified, **Cui loco, per deos immortales, iudices, consulite** *the situation*, Cic. *i Verr.* 15 43. So often **reipublicae, rei familiari, tempori** etc., and abstract words with **vaco, pateo** etc.

To instances of transitive verbs of helping may be added **medendis corporibus** Livy viii 36 7.

30. The Ethic Dative or dative of interest. **Nec longo deinde moranti Tempore contactos artus sacer ignis edebat** Virg. *Geo.* iii 566: **huc mihi...vir gregis ipse caper deerraverat** *Ec.* 7 6. A special use is that of the person judging: **pares aestimantibus** Liv. vii 10 6. By an idiom this becomes the main predicate (see **sec. 2 predicate**): **ut quibusque bellum volentibus vel cupientibus erat** Tac. *Ann.* i 59.

31. A dative of External Direction often follows a combination of **Noun and Verb**: **domicilio locum delegerunt** Caes. *b.g.* ii 29 5: **huic comitem mittit** Virg. *Aen.* xii 362: **signum mittendis quadrigis dare** Liv. viii 40 2: **oleas esui condire** Varro *R. R.* (Roby): **dare locum suspicioni** Cic. *pro Cael.* 4 9: **heres est fratri** *Fam.* xiii 26: **finem venisse Romano imperio** Liv. ii 45 10: **Causa fuit pater his** Hor. *Sat.* i 6 71: **architectu'st hominibus** Plaut. *Amph.* 45: **quid modi flendo facies** *Mil.* 1311. Virgil has also the following: **patet isti ianua leto** *Aen.* ii 661: **Coeo sororem progenuit** iv 179: **vitulam lectori pascite** *Ec.* 3 85: **stabulis furem horrebis** *Geo.* iii 407: **centurionem morti deposcit** Tac. *Ann.* i 23 6: add the Tacitean gerundives **Caecinam distrahendo hosti miserat** *Ann.* i 60 2: **partem prolis firmandae amicitiae miserat** ii 1: with **deligitur** ii 4 2: **finguntur** iv 1 4 (see **gerund** and **prolat. infin.**). **Receptui canere** with or without **signum** Cic. *Phil.* ii 3 8.

32. With Noun alone (External). **Collo monile** Virg. *Aen.* i 654: **collo decus aut capiti** x 135: **quis rebus dexter modus** iv 294: **suffugium hiemi et receptaculum frugibus** Tac. *G.* 16: **rector iuveni** *Ann.* i 24: **subsidia dominationi** *props to the throne* i 3: **liberis tutorem** ii 67: **seditioni duces** i 22: **paci firmator** ii 46: **descensus Averno** Virg. *Aen.* vi 126: **pro remedio aegris rebus** Livy ix 20 5: **causas bello** Tac. *Ann.* ii 64: **receptui signum (audire)** Cic. *Ph.* xiii 7 15: **linteum extersui** Plaut. *Curc.* 578: **muli vecturae** Cic. *Att.* xv 18 1. **Ostentui** is used by Tacitus in apposition: **corpora extra vallum abiecta ostentui** *Ann.* i 29: **vivere iubet [Meherdatem] ostentui clementiae suae** xii 14. The dative **frugi** has become an adjective.

To this belongs the dative gerundive of office or function as in **comitia tribunis creandis, triumviri agris dividendis.**

33. Predicative Dative (Internal Direction). An abstract noun is here actively or passively identified with a concrete noun preceding. **Auxilio esse** and **auxilio mittere** need not be separated. **Usu, mancipio dare** Lucr. iii 971: **noxae** or **noxiae dedere** Liv. xxvi 29 4, *to give up as a criminal*: more commonly **noxiae esse. Dare crimini** *impute as a fault* is different from **dare locum crimini** (external) above. **Fenori dare** *employ as a profitable loan* Cic. *ii Verr.* ii 70 170. A dative of the object is commonly added, rarely a genitive, as **Faliscorum auxilio venerunt** Liv. iv 17 11. A third dative in Cic. *Fam.* iii 10 6 **Ubi enim cuiquam legationi fui impedimento?** [**Dicto audiens** as predicate with another dative Roby 1163.]

NOTES ON DATIVE OF THE PREDICATE

34. [Note (*a*). Such abstract predicates are naturally seldom used with epithets, and then only with the simplest adjectives; as, **bonae frugi, minori usui, minori curae.** A peculiar use is with **nullo** not **nulli**, perhaps a survival of an old declension found in **alius** etc.: **nullo adiumento esse** Cic. *ii Verr.* v 40 103.

35. Note (*b*). The nominative is used without much difference in meaning in **religio est, operae pretium est, mos, cura fuit** sec. 134: **donum dare** as well as **dono dare, tutamentum fuerit** Liv. xxi 61 10: **praecipuum argumen-**

tum est Tac. *Germ.* 35 and **pretium fuit** *Ann.* i 57: **Momentumque fuit mutatus Curio rerum** Lucan ii 819. In Virg. *Ec.* 5 32 both **decori** and **decus** are predicated. In apposition: **liberti, raro aliquod momentum** Tac. *Germ.* 25: **rorarios minus roboris** Liv. viii 8 8.

Note (*c*). The use of abstract words for concrete seems to grow commoner in late Latin: as, **cenatio** for **cenaculum** which received another meaning: **gestatio** etc. for parts of the house: but otherwise as a rule Latin avoids identifying the concrete with the abstract: hence such phrases as **in pretio esse, in bonis habere** (ἐν ἀνδράσι Eur. *Alc.* 732): **in parte pari esse** *to share* Liv. vi 37 4 (in partem vocare): or again, **pro incommodo habere** *to count as a misfortune.*]

ABLATIVE CASE

36. The meaning of the case commonly so called is Sociative-Instrumental rather than Ablative or Locative. Where Locative or Ablative forms are used they have lost their distinctive meaning, and the ideas of place have to be supplied by prepositions or the form of the phrase, as **summo monte, pellere Italiâ.**

37. Association and Instrument. In the former the relation is mutual, in the latter simple: in practice they are hard to separate: *e.g.* **madidâ cum veste gravatum** and **veste gravis**: **comitatus Achate** and **armatis obsidet**: **tenere se castris** *to keep within the limits of camp* and **tutari se castris** *to shelter oneself by means of it.*

38. The Abl. of Association expressing fulness and the contrary. **Vaco** abl. always, sometimes with **ab**: **abundo** abl., gen. in Lucilius. **Saturo** abl. except in Plautus (Riem. p. 113 for others): **levo, careo, privo; egeo** and **indigeo** both also gen. **Compleo** abl., **completus** sometimes gen. Abl. usually with **impleo** (gen. seems colloquial; once in Cicero's letters), **nudo, nudus** and **orbus** (gen. in poets). **Immunis** abl. or gen. **Inanis aliquâ re** Cic. *Att.* ii 8 1; gen. in poetry. **Inops verbis** abl. of respect (**42**), also gen. as Cic. *Br.* 70 247. **Inflammavit amore** *Aen.* iv 54: **tollere honoribus** Hor. *Od.* i 1 8.

Other forms of Association are those with **contentus, comitatus, assuefactus** (**scelerum exercitatione** Cic. *Cat.* ii 5 9, otherwise dative: **assuefacio ad** Liv. iii 52 5: **assuetus labore** or dative): **coniunctus** (cele-

ritas venustate coniuncta Cic. *de Or.* i 57 243) or dat.; **misceo** (**faece Falernâ vina** Hor. *Sat.* ii 4 55) or **cum**: perhaps **cavis celebrabant orgia cistis** Cat. lxiv 259: **haeret pede pes densusque viro vir** *Aen.* x 361: **sese mucrone induit** 681: **valle resedit** viii 232: **solio, tecto invitare, solio sedere: mutare pacem bello** *peace for war* or *war for peace*: doubtful instances under **Abl. of Instrument**, **sec. 56–7**.

39. Abl. of Separation (dissociation): usually with prepositions and words which themselves denote separation, so that the ablative is the same as the above: **loco concedere alicui: vertere fundo.** Taking away generally governs the dative (*ôter à quelqu'un*), as, **adimo, arceo pecori** Virg. *G.* iii 155: **classibus depulit** *Aen.* v 726: **exemit Drusum dicendae primo loco sententiae** Tac. *Ann.* iii 22: **ut cunctos infamiae se ipsos morti eximant hortatur** i 48. **Eripio** dative or **ab**; **abl.** alone in poets. **Arceo, prohibeo, pello, moveo** regular with abl.: **arceo** also with **ab**: **demo** with **de.** In Livy **repello, revoco** have simple ablative; so in Virgil **Ductores acie revocaveris ambo** *Geo.* iv 88. **Procul** abl. in Livy: **haud procul hoste** ix 32 5. For **alienus** see under **Dative case 24.**

Compound verbs of departing often repeat the preposition **ab** or **ex,** which is always allowable even with the others: **ab Alexandriâ discedere** Cic. *Att.* xi 17 (below).

40. The following take abl. of the thing: **supersedeo** *do without*, **interdico** *forbid*, **invideo** *grudge* (genitive in Hor. *S.* ii 6 84); (**sibi**) **tempero** and (**se**) **abstineo** *refrain from*. **Se abstinere** usually with **ab** but also without **se** or **ab**: **abstineo** acc. rei Plaut. *Aul.* 345.

With places not considered as towns a preposition is required, as **ex Miseno, ab Appi foro**: **Tusculo ex urbe,** but **ipsâ Samo.** Virgil has **urbe reportat** *Geo.* i 275. **Domo tuâ** (Cic. *ii Verr.* v 30 77) or **a domo tuâ** (l. dub.) 15 38 (**extrudere**). Livy uses **ab** with towns, but usually meaning *from the neighbourhood of*, or of distance or view from a town. Dates of letters usually abl., rarely locative (**59**).

For **Depriving** see above **sec. 38**: **secreta cibo** and **teporis** Lucr.

41. Standard of Act or Judgment. **Legibus licet** *the law permits*: **meâ sententiâ** *as far as my opinion goes*: **pretio non aequitate iura discribere** Cic. *ii Verr.* v 11 27: **discriptus populus censu** *leg.* iii 19 44: **utilitate officium dirigi** *Off.* ii 23 89: **voluntate eius** *Att.* x 10 1. So of the standard in valuing, not the value itself: **aestimarent Sidicinorum cladibus Samnitium virtutem** Liv. vii 32 7 (**fructibus et utilitate amicitiam colere** Cic. *Fin.* ii 26 83 is of standard rather than cause, **sec. 55**).

Fidibus canere: **aleâ ludere**: **tenere se castris** (52 (*c*)))(**tutari se castris**: **pacto, promissis stare**: **suo quisque fato vivent** Liv. ix 18 19: esp. of the matter of a contest: **cursibus auras vocat** Virg. *Geo.* iii 193: **ventos lacessit ictibus** *challenges to a match in buffets, ib.*: **fatis aperit ora** *Aen.* ii 246. **Ordine, ratione, naturâ, forte,** usually classed under manner, should be placed here, and those marked under **49.**

42. Ablative of Respect, or measure of fact. **Fallitque timor regione viarum** Virg. *Aen.* ix 385: **temporibus errasti** Cic. *Ph.* ii 9 23: **ingenio pollere**: **numero comparare** (or above): **tantum bello virum**: **urbs Etrusca solo** Virg. *Aen.* x 180: **haud mollia fatu** xi 25 and other supines in **-u**: compare **levis cursu.** Cicero hardly distinguishes this use from instrument in **Utrum ista classis cursu et remis an sumptu tantum et litteris navigarit** *pro Flacc.* 14 32 (*really sailed or on paper*): **beneficio gratum** *Phil.* ii 46 117 *grateful in respect of service rendered*: **omnibus rebus** *in all respects*: **altero oculo capitur** Liv. xxi 2 11: **oculis constare** v 42 3: **animo dissidere** Cic. *ii Verr.* v 71 182: **pondo** *in weight* (**iii pondo** 3 *pounds*): **Cn. Lentulus non tardus sententiis sed inops verbis** *Brut.* 70 247: **verbis se locupletem faceret** *made out as far as words went* not *by words Flacc.* 20 46.

43. Abl. of Comparison. This may be regarded as signifying a standard, which connects it with the abl. of **Association.** Note **dicto celerius** *no sooner said than done*: **opinione celerius** *unexpectedly soon.* **Quo nihil maius meliusve terris Fata donavere** Hor. *Od.* iv 2 37 (the regular way of expressing *greatest on earth* though Livy has **celerrimae totâ classe, fortissimi toto exercitu** xxvi 38), and Cic. **maximi inter homines** *Att.* viii 11 1. An abbreviation follows **quam** as in Greek: **neminem vidi callidiorem quam Phormionem** Ter. *Phorm.* iv 21: but also **quam Phormio est. Alius Lysippo** abl. as **alium sapiente bonoque** Hor. *Ep.* i 16 20. **Par** and **impar** in Ovid take abl., **Facies par nobilitate suâ** Ovid *Fast.* vi 804 and **aeque** in Plautus. A *comparative genitive* appears possibly in **horum secundus** Cic. *Or.* 1 4. *Ellipse of* **quam** with the ablative case occurs in Hor., **Mero pontificum potiore cenis** *Od.* ii 14 28: and **Mollivit aversos penates (non blandior) Farre pio et saliente micâ** iii 23 20. **Supremâ citius die** i 13 20.

Plus and **minus** (**sec. 58**) are used with numbers in unaltered case as **Plus sexcenti cecidere: plus** (**amplius**) **novem annos natus** (also **plus xxx annis natus** in Plautus). **Pluris unius assis** Hor. *S.* i 6 14: **Noctem non amplius unam** Virg. *Aen.* 1 683: **neque enim plus septima ducitur aestas** *Geo.* iv 207. **Ne plus sit annuum** Cic. *Att.* v 1 1. **Maior** and **minor** more rarely: **annos natus maior quadraginta** Cic. *pro Rosc. Am.* 14 39: **res minor lx milium** *of less than* Tac. *Ann.* iv 63: **boves minores trimos** Varr. *R. R.* 1 20.

44. Ablative (and Genitive) of Crime. If the Locative is used of penalty as partly appears, the offence is best considered abl. of Association (respect). **Quo scelere damnatus** Cic. *Ph.* xiii 12 27: **Damnabis tu quoque votis** Virg. *Ec.* 5 80. **Lege** and **crimine** are used by Cic. together, also **criminibus** and **testibus. Capite** *on a capital charge* is found as well as **capitis** whether it represent penalty or crime: the latter more probable from the old phrase **capitis anquirere. Capitis minor** in Hor. (*Od.* iii 5 42) which is later seems to be imitated from **capite deminutus** (Liv. xxii 60 15) and therefore represents penalty.

45. Ablative of Quality with Epithet. Domus sanie dapibusque cruentis Virg. *Aen.* iii 618 is a violent hendiadys. The abl. of quality expresses external or temporary characteristics, the genitive permanent traits: *e.g.* **bono animo este,** but **vir animi egregii.** Or the abl. may express habitual or permanent external traits. **Capillo sunt promisso atque omni parte corporis rasâ** Caes. *b.g.* v 14 3: or a real quality now manifested, as, **egregiâ virtute erant cogniti** (*found to be of*) i 28 5. **Stellis nebulam spargere candidis** Hor. *Od.* iii 15 6 coincides with abl. of manner which qualifies an act. **Quo genere** *even as* (of a class observed) Lucr. **Duplici numero classem** Liv. xxiv 36 7. **Te praestanti prudentiâ virum, maximi animi hominem** Cic. *Fam.* iv 8: the man in action and the man in himself. So **novo quodam genere imperator** *ii Verr.* v 12 29 though some read **ex genere. Quâ facie quâ staturâ** *Phil.* ii 16 41 facts in evidence: but **exstinctae corpus non utile dextrae** of a permanent and vital disablement Juv. iii 48.

46. Virgil by an inverted construction turns this abl. into one of respect: **saxis suspensam rupem** Virg. *Aen.* viii 190 for **saxis suspensis: gravis ictu** v 274, stronger than **gravi ictu: plurimus imbre descendit** (Jupiter) *Ecl.* 7 60 for the commonplace **plurimo.**

With names **vir** or **homo** is usually added: but **Philippus summâ nobilitate** Cic. *Planc.* 21 52: **non iuniores modò sed emeritis stipendiis** Liv. iii 57 9.

Ablative of Origin and Material is a special form of the above, though often replaced by abl. with **ex** and **de. Humili loco ortus, matre musâ natus**: still closer **equestri natu homo**: but also **natus ex patre libertino.**

47. There need be no word of origin. **Serv. Sulpicius Lemoniâ (tribu), N. Magius Cremonâ, Verres Romiliâ, iuvenis hinc. Maeoniâ generose domo** Virg. *Aen.* x 141 combines origin and quality. Livy uses name of town with **ab: Turnus Herdonius ab Ariciâ.** The name of a country has **ex: C. Iunius ex Hispaniâ.**

Of Quality also are **loco, numero parentis** etc. with **esse.**

48. Ablative of Manner and Circumstance. This only differs from Quality in the governing verb. A word of quality cannot be used alone. Note the military expressions **adesse omnibus copiis, magno comitatu venire, exiguis copiis pugnare**; also an external form of circumstance in **Quĕrelis haud iustis adsurgis** Virg. *Aen.* x 95: **saltus maiore pernicie superatus** Liv. xxi 35 1: **ingenti militum alacritate** vi 8 10.

49. Cum adds emphasis even with an adjective, though not then necessary. **Cum meo maximo dolore** *to my very great grief.* **Madidâ cum veste gravatum** Virg. *Aen.* vi 359 *heavy with his wet garments about him.* **Ille suo cum gurgite flavo Accepit venientem** *took him to his golden breast* ix 816.

Cum however is not necessary with an adjective. **Pulcherrimo vestitu sedens** Cic. *de fin.* ii 21 69. **Bonâ tuâ veniâ. Meo maximo periculo.** All these might equally well have **cum.** The epithet may be replaced by a genitive, attributive or possessive; **auspiciis, ductu, vice alicuius: more ferae, loco parentis, duarum cohortium damno** Caes. *b. g.* vi 44 1: **vasarii nomine** Cic. *in Pis.* xxxv 86 *on the score of furniture*, **discessu, rogatu, iussu alicuius: captorum habitu ingressi** Liv. ix 7 10.

Single words without epithet express a circumstance only, not a principle: the former include **gemitu** Virg.: **clamore** Tac. and Virg.; **silentio** (**accipere** and **praeterire**): to **41** belong **precario** *on sufferance*, **vitio** *informally*, **insidiis** *treasonably*, **iure** *rightfully* and **iniuriâ** *wrongfully*, **fraude** or **fraude malâ** *guiltily*, **furto, sponte, cursu, pedibus, agmine,** and **lege** with **agere**.

Manner may be expressed by **per. Per vim** *violently*, **per timorem** *in fear*, **per silentium** *in silence.*

50. Ablative Absolute. This convenient name, which only means released from rules, is given to some *concrete ablatives of circumstance.* It may denote effect as well as circumstance: **fide incolumi creditum solvi** Liv. vi 15 5: **quantis se attollet gloria rebus** Virg. *Aen.* iv 49. It should seldom be rendered literally. The English participle corresponds with **dum** or **quum** in Latin and has itself no flexibility.

The participle or its equivalent may stand alone; as, **sortito** Cic. *ii Verr.* ii 51 126: **libato** Virg. *Aen.* i 737: **composito rumpit vocem** ii 129: **explorato egressus, edicto ut, excepto quod, nondum comperto utrum; libero quid firmaret** Tac. *Ann.* iii 60: **nec auspicato nec litato, necopinato; non distincto suâ an alienâ manu** xi 38.

51. Similarly the adjective may stand alone; **tranquillo silet** Virg. *Aen.* v 127; **iuxta periculoso ficta seu vera promeret** Tac. *Ann.* i 6.

Or the noun: as in **bello, ludis, comitiis, Saturnalibus, terrâ marique,** and others. **Dedit iura quibus pace et principe uteremur** Tac. *Ann.* iii 28. **Vento rubet** Virg. *Geo.* i 431. So **morte Sychaei, Neoptolemi** *Aen.* iv 502 and iii 333 and the ordinary abl. of **Time.**

Noun and adjective together: **nobis invitis, bono imperatore, tanto conventu; tali re talique tempore** Cic. *Att.* xiv 19 5; **nullis nec Gallicis nec lacernâ** *Phil.* ii 30 76: **salvâ dignitate: incolumi Iove et urbe Româ** Hor. *Od.* iii 5 12: **hoc caelo** Virg. *Aen.* v 18. **Noun and noun**: **me puero; duce et auspice Teucro** Hor. *Od.* i 7 27.

Noun understood: **quibus quisque poterat elatis** Liv. i 29 3.

In Virgil the perfect participle is not uncommon to denote circumstance or even place without time, owing to the want of a present passive form. **Stat ductis sortibus urna** *Aen.* vi 22: **magnis Circensibus actis** viii 636 *at the holding of the games*: **vectis** *on a voyage*, *Geo.* i 206: **tenebrosa palus Acheronte refuso** *Aen.* vi 107 *where Acheron flows back*: **terram invertere satis dentibus** *Geo.* ii 141: **campum fractis invertere glebis** iii 160: **exercitum accipiunt parte militum dimissa novisque adductis** Liv. ix 24 1. Accordngly it may even denote a result. In **plures diffluit partes, multis ngentibusque insulis effectis** (*en formant*: Fr.) Caes. *b. g.* iv 10 3: **usque ad lucem proelio abstinuerunt...eo tempore absumpto** *and spent the time* Liv. xxi 49 11: **hebetes lasso lictore secures** Juv. viii 137: **pulsatos infecto foedere divos** *Aen.* xii 286.

The abl. abs. is used with **quasi** and **tanquam** for a comparative clause: **tanquam non transituris in Asiam Romanis** Liv. xxxvi 41: **quasi praedâ sibi advectâ** Cic. *ii Verr.* v 25 64: **nisi** after neg. *Fam.* i 4 1: **quanquam** Sall. *Jug.* 43 1.

Ablatives expressing limit, or measurement by a concrete standard:

52. (*a*) Road traversed: **viâ Appiâ ire: equites finibus Frisiorum duxit** Tac. *Ann.* i 60 2: **ut mutato itinere iugis Octogesam perveniret** Caes. *b. c.* i 70 5: **obliquo monte** Liv. vii 15 5: **pelago trahit** Virg. *Geo.* i 142: **portis egressus** *by* not *from the gates*: **rectâ pergere in exsilium** Cic. *Cat.* i 9 23. Perhaps the phrase **nostrâ refert** *it points in the direction of our interests* belongs here. All this may coincide with (*c*).

(*b*) Distance measured: **distat intervallo: milibus passuum duobus hinc, ultrà Caesarem: leti discrimine parvo Esse suos** *Aen.* x 511. See further under Measure of Difference. The Cognate accusative is also used.

(*c*) Space inclusive: **totâ urbe: fortissimi toto exercitu** Liv. xxvi 38 12: and in Virgil **omnibus aris: micat ore linguis: mandet humo solitâ** *Aen.* ix 214: **fluminibus salices** *Geo.* ii 110: **terrâ marique** or either separately: **tenere se castris** given above: perhaps **summo monte, celsâ sedet Aeolus arce** and poetical ablatives of Place: **campo** and **litore** Tac. *Ann.* iv 74 12.

(*d*) Time measured is similar to distance measured: **tribus antè** or **abhinc horis,** and **ante diem tertium.**

(*e*) Time inclusive. The outside limit is given, and the occupation is not necessarily continuous, even when **totus** is used. **Nocte ac die bina castra hostium expugnata** Liv. xxv 39 11. **Quinque diebus nil erat in loculis** *in five days or less* Hor. *S.* i 3 17. **Bis anno. Nocte custodita castra** Liv. ix 42 6. **Hieme** or **hiemis spatio.** But the idiom came to be used of the identical duration of act and time. **Totis Quinquatribus optat** (*any time during*) Juv. x 115. **Quae duabus aestatibus gesta coniunxi** (*at various periods during*)

Tac. *Ann.* vi 38. So **reliquis itineribus** Caes. *b. c.* i 24 4. But **Quinque horis proelium sustinuissent** (Caes. *b. c.* i 47 3) means *five hours out and out.* **Quot Acestes vixerit annis** (Juv. vii 235) is the regular form in late Latin, and lays stress on the exact duration of life. **Quattuordecim annis exilium toleravit** Tac. *Ann.* i 53. **Octoginta annis vixit** in Seneca (*ep.* 93 3): **vixit annis xxix imperavit triennio** (Suet. *Cal.* 59) might suggest *so much and no more.* Especially the abl. is used of a period in which something does not happen or rarely happens: **unus tot annis inventus. Multis annis non venit** Cic. *Rosc. Am.* 27 74.

In is commonly used: **in horâ saepe ducentos dictabat versus** Hor. *Sat.* i 4 9. (**Quae inter decem annos nefariè facta sunt** Cic. *i Verr.* 13 37.)

53. (*f*) **Measure of difference**, especially with comparatives and superlatives, and with verbs of comparison. Besides **eo, quo, quanto** etc. add **impendio** colloquial, **spatio, intervallo, toto caelo (discrepare), altero tanto maior, quinquiens tanto, uno plures, duabus partibus maior, quî melius? Non die non horâ citius** Liv. ix 34 15. This abl. is used with **ante** and **post** but seldom with their compounds: with **disto** and **absum** only when a noun is used: **longè abest** but **tribus milibus (tria milia) abest. Longè** is often for **multo** with comparatives and superlatives and such words as **praesto.** With **praesto multo** and **maxime** are also used. Livy writes **aliquantum ampliorem. Quantum iuniores se magis insinuabant** Liv. iii 15 2 to avoid ambiguity. This ablative is used by Tacitus without any comparison expressed. **Eo interritus** *Ann.* i 64: **quanto intentus...tanto resolutus** iv 67: **apud turbidos eoque nova cupientes: poena admodum vi tractata, quo ceteris quies esset** (187).

54. Ablative of Instrument. This includes the common use of the **abl. of the gerund.**

In poetry sometimes **ab** is used with the Instrument. **Pisces captantur ab hamis** Ovid *A. A.* i 763. **Intritae ab labore** Caes.

b. g. iii 26 2. **Constare** *to consist of* is not used with abl. in the best prose; but **parvo fames constat** *is secured by little* and therefore *costs little* develops into abl. of price. **Facere vitulâ** in the sense of *sacrificing*.

55. Ablative of the Cause.

This is of the same nature as Abl. of Instrument but is used with verbs denoting State. It is less common than the accusative with **propter. Saevus ubi Aeacidae telo iacet Hector** Virg. *Aen.* i 99. **Suis testibus iacent** Cic. *pro Mil.* 18 47. It is also used of the motive or reason of an act or the cause which prevents it (equivalent to **prae**). **Quâ re** *wherefore* (**quibus rebus**). **Levitate armorum nihil eis noceri posse** Caes. *b. g.* v 34 3. **Neque ipse manus feritate dedisset** Virg. *Aen.* xi 568. Perhaps also **macte virtute esto** (**esse**) though it might be abl. of respect. (**Fructibus et utilitate amicitiam colere** Cic. *Fin.* ii 26 83, *on the grounds of profit* etc., = **fructuum et utilitatis causâ**, or *by the standard of profit*, **sec. 41**.)

[**Per** expresses a means or an obstacle not a cause: **per me stat** *I hinder*, **per me licet** *I do not forbid*. **Prae** gives the cause preventing: **solem prae iaculorum multitudine non videbitis** Cic. *Tusc.* i 42 101.]

56. The Instrument or Associate may be a person. In that case instrument and association hardly differ: it is not entirely poetical. **Assiduo ruptae lectore columnae** Juv. *Sat.* i 13. **Inaequali curatus tonsore** Hor. *Ep.* i 1 94. **Uno comitatus Achate** Virg. *Aen.* i 312. **Meis excisus Argivis** Hor. *Od.* iii 3 67. **Uxore paene constrictus** with other (instrumental) ablatives in Cic. *pro Mil.* 20 54. **Facilius crediderim Tiberio et Augustâ cohibitam** Tac. *Ann.* iii 3 is a doubtful reading: there is no certain instance of a deliberate *agent* without **ab**, though **Vario** in Hor. *Od.* i 6 1 is certainly abl. and it is hard to believe it an abl. abs. (perhaps instrumental, *you may get V. to write*). **Dominis Cirrhae Nisaeque feruntur** Juv. vii 64, as we say possessed *with* a demon. **Meis lecticariis eum in urbem referre** Servilius in Cic.

Fam. iv 12. **Testibus laeditur** Cic. *Q. f.* 3 3. **Agros turpissimis possessoribus inquinavit** Cic. *Ph.* ii 17 43. **Punicâ classe vastari** Liv. **Stipatus armatis: cavere praedibus: deseror coniuge** Ov. (assoc.). **Quid hoc homine faciatis?** Cic. *ii Verr.* i 16 42. **Quid me fiet?** (or **de me**). **Si quid Pompeio factum esset** Cic. *de imp.* 20 59.

57. Fungor etc. The abl. is instrumental or sociative. **Potior** *make oneself strong with* or *by*. See **Middle Voice** (100). **Vescor** *live on* or *by*. So **fretus**: but **fretus, contentus** under **Association.** As to the usage, **fungor, fruor** etc., are transitive in comedy and in Lucretius: Tac. has **hominum officia fungi** *Ann.* iv 38: **fruendus, fungendus, potiendus** and **utendus** occur in Livy and Cicero: and **potior** governs the genitive also, as in Cic. *Off.* iii 32 113: compare **apiscor, adipiscor** with genitive in Tacitus. **Compos** abl. occurs in Livy: elsewhere genitive. **Dignus** and **indignus** as well as **opus** and **usus** sometimes take the genitive. **Indignus avorum** Virg. *Aen.* xii 649, and in colloquial prose as Balbus in Cic. *Att.* viii 15 A. 1. **Temporis opus esse** Liv. xxii 51 3. **Usus operae sit** xxvi 9: besides **dux nobis et auctor opus est** Cic. *Fam.* ii 6. The verb after **opus** is in the perfect not the gerund: as, **maturato, properato opus est. Opus fuit Hirtio convento** Cic. *Att.* x 4. **Dictu opus est** Ter. *Haut.* 941: **scitu** in Cic. *de Inv.* i 20. **Quod te scire opus est** Cic. *Q. f.* ii 9; rarely in the plural **haec opus sunt.** In Cato there is a combination of personal and impersonal: **quae opus sient locato locentur** *R. R.* 2. **Quid opus est facto** in comedy: compare **quid tibi hanc tactio est?** (sec. 21). Add **fido** abl. of things, **diffido** late.

58. Ablatives of Price, Value and Penalty. The 'genitive sing.' and 'abl. pl.' may perhaps be considered locatives. **Pluris** and **minoris** perhaps by a false analogy: on the other hand the real ablative is certainly found for value as well as for price and penalty. Taking the cases as we find them, the abl. is used of definite price. **Emat denario quod sit mille denarium** Cic. *de Off.* iii 23 92 (63). **Arcem scelere emptam** Liv. i 12 4: **mercede**

conducere (**pacisci** Liv. xxv 33 3): **fenore sumere** and **accipere** *tc invest* and *borrow at interest*: of definite penalty in **morte condemnare, multare exsilio, morte, pecuniâ** (or **-ae**), **agro, stipendio.** Rarely of proportionate penalty: **quadruplo** Cic. *ii Verr.* iii 13 34. Rarely of the act of valuing, but so with **aestimare.** Of indefinite price, **vili, parvo, magno, plurimo, minimo** and **impenso.** The ablative would be Instrumental: **parvo constat** literally is *secured by little* and so *costs little* (**sec. 54** above). For **capite** see **44.**

LOCATIVE CASE

59. **Rure** is poetical for **ruri** besides its regular use as abl. *from the country.* **Rure meo** *on my estate* Hor. is ablative, like **summo monte.** **Domi fratris** and **domi tuae, alienae** Cic. *Fam.* iv 7 4: **in domo meâ** *in my town house.* **Militiae** *on service*, **belli** *in war*, **peregre** *abroad* or *from abroad*, **foris** *out of doors* or *from without*, **humi** *on* or *to the ground*, **vesperi** not **vespere** in prose. **Non Libyae non ante Tyro** Virg. *Aen.* iv 36: **Cretae considere** iii 162: **Karthagini** or **Karthagine,** but **Tibure** seldom **Tiburi**: **Suessae Auruncae**: **in ipsâ Alexandriâ** Cic. *Att.* xi 16 1: **in urbe Româ** or **Romae in urbe**: **Antiochiae, urbe celebri** *Arch.* iii 4. Letters are dated abl., rarely loc.

Add to locatives perhaps **cordi** *at heart* (or *dat. of predicate* **sec. 63**), **macte animi** *be of good cheer*: but see under **Genitive** (**74**).

In expressions *of Time* we find **quotīdie, merīdie, prīdie, postrīdie** or **die posteri, die septimi, crastini, proximi** (old), **luci.**

The Locative of Value and Penalty has become lost in the abl. and genitive. See under **Abl. of Price** and **Genitive of Value, 58, 64.**

Place otherwise requires a preposition in good prose even after **inesse,** except with some compounds of **ad** and **inter, sec. 11.**

Apparent exceptions with abl. **sec. 38, 52.**

GENITIVE CASE

60. The Genitive Case (γενικὴ not γεννητική) signifies **Class not Origin.** It expresses the relation of thing, person or class to an identical or other thing, person or class; it also defines a thought, feeling or state expressed by verbs and adjectives. It may also express a Class Qualified.

A. 61. External relation to a thing or person. **Possessive Genitive.** The possessive adjectives take the place of the personal pronouns. Note **solius meum peccatum** Cic. *Att.* xi 15 and comp. **Pugna Romana...incumbentium in hostem** Liv. xxx 34 2: **Noster duorum eventus** vii 9 8. Various relations besides possession will be included: **Diodorus Timarchidi** Cic.: **mucro gladii**: **pretium operae**: **pridie postridie eius diei**: **dies, tempus comitiorum**: **pugna Cannarum** (usually **Cannensis**) Liv. xxiii 43 4: **tutelae nostrae duximus** xxi 41 12: **ornamenta quae sunt loci huius** Cic. *Att.* i 6: **da lunae propere novae, da, puer, auguris Murenae** (**poculum**) Hor. *Od.* iii 19 10: **cyathos amici Sospitis** iii 8 13: **neque gloriam meam laborem illorum faciam** *claim the glory and leave them the drudgery* Sall. *Jug.* 85 34. **Sacer, proprius, communis, alienus** govern this genitive, but see **sec. 24.** (**Subjective Genitive**: **dei munus**: **spes surgentis Iuli** *hope inspired by Iulus' future* Virg. *Aen.* vi 364 [or it might be **Objective, sec. 71**]. **Genitive of the Author. Totum muneris hoc tui est Quod monstror digito praetereuntium** Hor. *Od.* iv 3 21: **signum Myronis.**)

B. 62. External relation to a Class different from the governing word (**Attributive Genitive**). A separate class is often but not always expressed in the plural: **lux solis** *light of a sun* or *sunlight*: **hospitis adfectu** *with hospitable zeal* Juv. viii 161: **specie festinantis**: on the other hand **delphinum caudas utero commissa luporum** of one monster Virg. *Aen.* iii 428. **Fallax herba veneni** Virg. *Ec.* 4 24: outwardly similar to **lacte veneni**

under D (see **67**) below. Further instances are found under the **Gerundive**: **oratores pacis petendae** etc.

As predicate: **pars philosophiae quae est quaerendi** Cic. *Fin.* i 7 22: **duas partes tironum esse** Liv. xxii 41 5: **fies...fontium** Hor. *Od.* iii 13 13: **nil mortalibus ardui est** i 3 37: **cetera quae sunt gymnasii** (*suitable for*) Cic. *Att.* i 8 2: **dubitare quin meus discessus desperationis sit** xv 20 1.

So with the object of a verb: **compendi facere** *to make short work of*, or *make light of*: **lucri facere** *count as gain* Cic. *Flacc.* 37 91, **boni consulere** *take in good part* Ov. *Trist.* iv 1 106: **nihil reliqui facere** Tac. *Ann.* i 21, Sall. *Cat.* 11 *to leave nothing undone*: **neque fas neque fidem pensi haberet** Tac. *Ann.* xiii 15.

Tacitus is fond of quaint attributive genitives: **Sacerdotium hominum** *a blasphemous priesthood*, *Ann.* i 59: **effigie numinum** *a divine image* ii 69: **insignia lugentium** *garb of mourning* ii 82. The governing word is often abstract, as well as the genitive, which may then be classed under D, **sec. 69**. For others see **sec. 144**.

63. Genitive of Quality (including Number and Age) *with epithet*: distinguished from the ablative by denoting permanent characteristics: as, **multi cibi hospitem** *a voracious guest*, not incidentally but always Cic. *Fam.* 9 26: **exstinctae corpus non utile dextrae** Juv. iii 48: **naves sui quisque commodi fecerat** Caes. *b. g.* v 8 6 (*ships to suit*). Of persons usually with **vir** or **homo**; but **Eiusdem properabat Acilius aevi** Juv. iv 94: **T. Manlius priscae severitatis** Liv. xxii 60 5. Further instance **res mei arbitrii** (**est** or alone) Liv. IX 9 9.

64. Number and Age. **Classis triginta navium**: **iter tridui**: **puer novem annorum**: or directly with verb: **Fabius moritur exactae aetatis** Liv. xxx 26 7: **novem annorum profectus** xxx 37 9: **novem annorum natus** inscr. Further under cognate acc. and abl. of comparison (**19**, **43**).

Value and Penalty: **teruncii** *at a farthing*: **magni interest** (also **magnopere** and **multum**): **flocci, lucri, parvi, compendi,**

facere *to account as a gain, a trifle* etc. The genitive includes indefinite price as well as value: for the rest see end of abl. case (**sec. 58**). The genitive is used in proportionate penalties: **damnare minoris, octupli** (also **quadruplo**): also **capitis** (but see **44**): **capitalis poenae** Liv. xlii 43 9. (In Cic. *i Verr.* i 13 **minoris damnari** is *to be convicted at less expense.*)

65. The Genitive of Crime is a true Attributive genitive, governed perhaps by a noun idea inherent in the verb, as it is in **reum facere, damnare crimine parricidii.** Compare **compertus flagitii** Tac. *Ann.* i 3: **sceleris purus** Hor. *Od.* i 22 1: and conversely **notus** (*i.e.* **laudatus**) **animi paterni** ii 2 6. Or it may be akin to the genitives with **pudet** etc. (**73**). Compare **Iustitiaene prius mirer belline laborum?** Virg. *Aen.* xi 126. (For the **Abl. of Crime** see under that case **sec. 44.**) The genitive of the gerundive is rarely used (of an attempted crime: **occupandae reipublicae argui** Tac. *Ann.* vi 10): its place is taken by the conjunctive with **quod** or **tanquam. Damnare pecuniae** is *to condemn to a fine* or *for a theft.* **Manifesta vitae** Tac. *Ann.* xii 51 is a distortion of **manifesta sceleris. Damnare voti** (**voti reus** Virg. *Aen.* v 237) *to condemn to pay a vow* by granting the condition. When there is difficulty or awkwardness about the genitive, other constructions are used: as, **de vi, inter sicarios, de ambitu.** For **capitis** see under **sec. 44.**

C. 66. Internal relation to a Class narrower than the governing word (**Defining Genitive**): **Regio viarum** Virg. *Aen.* xi 530: **oceani finem** iv 480: **aggeribus murorum** x 24: **spretae iniuria formae** *wrong done in despising beauty* (concrete in form) i 27: **praedae hominum pecudumque actae** Liv. xxiv 20 4: **magnâ de stirpe nepotum** Virg. *Aen.* vi 864: **signum 'optimae matris'** of a pass-word Quintilian ii 2 10: **causam amoris = amorem** Cic. *Ph.* ii 31 78 [**excusatio valetudinis** *Pis.* vi 13 would be 'external,' from **excusare valetudinem**]: **cultus deorum utrisque Dianam et Apollinem venerandi** Tac. *Ann.* i 63.

D. 67. Genitive of Class Qualified by governing word. When the genitive is concrete and the definition is one of number or quantity the genitive is commonly called **partitive**: as, **unus nostrum** (this form is used, not **nostri** etc.): **alter consulum**: **fortissima Tyndaridarum** Hor. *Sat.* i 1 100: **dulcissime rerum** i 9 4 [**omnium nostrum** uses the partitive form by analogy with **tres nostrum** etc.]: **frequentia vestrum** Cic. *Ph.* iv 1 1 for the usual **vestra.** To this head though not partitive belong **is splendor est vestrum** (not **vester**) *Att.* vii 13 3: **scelus viri!** *the scoundrel* Plaut. *Truc.* ii 7 60: **quid hoc est sceleris?** Ter. *Eun.* ii 3 34: **quid mulieris uxorem habes?** *Hec.* iv 4 21. Compare '*a jewel of a wife.*' Comp. perhaps **litterarum officium** *kind letter* Cic. *Fam.* vi 6 1. Perhaps **lacte veneni** *Aen.* iv 514 is *milky poison* rather than *poisonous milk.*

68. With pronouns and words of quantity there is no necessary thought of a part, but rather of a type. **Qui captivorum remissi ad suos fuerant** Liv. ii 22 6 *all prisoners* (not *the* prisoners) who had been sent home: **quod roboris fuit**: **quod erat militum.** **Agro Samniti...quod eius publicum esset** Liv. xxxi 4 2. **Rosa quo locorum sera moretur** Hor. *Od.* i 38 3. **Eodem est loci quo reliquisti** Cic. *Att.* i 13 5. **Mille nummum, hominum** for **mille homines** Liv.: rare in Cic.: **flumen sanguinis**: **sex dies spatii** Caes. *b. c.* i 3 5 (more commonly **spatium dierum xxx** Cic. *ii Verr.* ii 39 96 Genitive of Quality): **sextarius vini**: **quinque millia mercedis** *ii Verr.* iii 61 140: **expediti peditum** Liv. xxviii 14 16: **lucus abietis** not a wood consisting of pines but a whole wood of pine: **multum vini**: **satis laboris**: **num quid novi?** = *de nouveau* not *du nouveau*: **serum erat diei**: **quodcumque hoc regni** Virg. *Aen.* i 78: **adfatim est hominum**: **surgit amari aliquid** Lucr. iv 1134. (In **aliquid ex iniquo** Tac. *Ann.* xiv 44, **ex** is the preposition of identity not part.)

The governing neuter is rarely anything but subject or object of its sentence: as, **in immensum altitudinis** (rare). Third declension adjectives are usually in agreement; sometimes others also: as, **nihil tenue, nihil sordidum.** This genitive cannot govern another word, thus **nihil exspectatione dignum** not **digni.**

69. In adverbial expressions likewise the genitive is abstract not partitive: **id aetatis** *at that age*: **post id locorum** *after that time* Sall. *Jug.* 72: **adhuc locorum** Plaut. *Capt.* 385: **interea loci** Ter. *Eun.* 1 2 46: **postea loci** Sall. *Jug.* 102: **minime gentium** Ter. *Ad.* 3 2 44: **eo miseriarum** Sall. *Jug.* 14.

Many Tacitean genitives come under this head, though it is difficult to say whether they are more qualifying or qualified. **Angustiae itinerum** *Ann.* xv 43: **cetera aulae** i 7: **alia honorum** i 9: **uligines paludum** i 17: **inculta montium** *ib.*: **simulationum falsa** vi 45: **umido paludum** i 61: **multa duritiae** iii 34: **cuncta curarum** iii 35: **alia sumptuum** iii 52: **occulta saltuum** *forest fastnesses* i 61: **celeberrimo fori** iv 67 not partitive: so with **asperrimo hiemis** ii 5: **cetera Africae** iv 5 and **obstantia silvarum** i 50. This use is also found in Sallust and in Virgil (**strata viarum** *Aen.* i 422 from Lucretius), and in Cic. **omnia reliquorum ludorum** *Att.* xv 26 1: sing. **humi arido** Sall. *Jug.* 48 3.

70. The **Genitive of Mark** is a special case of the External Genitives A and B, denoting the person or character to which an act belongs, and may equally come under those headings. It may follow **proprium**, **vitium** etc. (**vitium senectutis est** Cic. *de Sen.* 11 35). **Cuiusvis hominis est errare** Cic. *Phil.* xii 2 5: **hoc doctoris intelligentis est** *Brut.* 56 204: **videtur esse sapientis** *Acad.* ii 3 9: **negavit moris esse Graecorum** *ii Verr.* i 26 66, also **mos erat** etc. commonly (**sec. 134**): **hoc sentire prudentiae est** *Sest.* 40 86: **meus discessus desperationis sit** *Att.* xv 20 1 (**operae est** for **operae pretium est** Enn. *ap.* Pers. vi 9 essentially the same genitive). **Fuit alterum gravitatis alterum prudentiae tuae** Cic. *Phil.* ii 10 24. **Id quoque morum Tiberii fuit** Tac. *Ann.* i 80. For the genitive of personal pronouns the possessive is used: **puto esse meum quidquid sentiam expromere** Cic. *Fam.* vi 5: agreeing with the infinitive in **Hoc ridere meum** Pers. *Sat.* i 122. As second predicate after a verb of thinking: **illam obsidionem flagitii ratus** Tac. *Ann.* iii 20: **saevum id malique moris visum** i 35. Add **muneris tui sec. 61.**

E. 71. Objective Genitive. This term is used rather ambiguously to denote both the object of a verbal idea in nouns and adjectives, and the object or matter of thought and feeling. In either case it belongs to A but is more convenient here. **Sunt lacrimae rerum** Virg. *Aen.* i 462 and **custos furum** *Geo.* iv 110 are instances. The possessive adjectives are occasionally used for the regular **nostri mei** etc. objective: **odio fecit tuo** Ter. *Phorm.* v 9 27: **suo periculo** Cic. *ii Verr.* v 20 50: **inimicus meus, accusator noster**; **habenda ratio non sua solum sed etiam aliorum** *Off.* i 39 139 side by side with **non modo deprecatorem sed etiam accusatorem mei** *Att.* xi 8. Tacitus uses the latter form with little objective sense in **longam sui absentiam** *Ann.* xii 37: so **sui cum periculo** Caes. *b. g.* iv 28 2 (unless **suo** is read): **sui causâ** Cic. *ii Verr.* iii 52 121 (reading again doubtful, but apparently to contrast with **Metelli**): **nostri nuntius esto** Virg. *Aen.* iv 237. Tacitus has regularly **iactantia sui** *Ann.* ii 46: **cultu sui** ii 58: Virgil **tui fidissima** *Aen.* xii 659. With nouns may be added **deorum opinio** belief in gods: **insolentia fori** Cic. *Rosc. Am.* 31 88. For clearness a preposition may be used: as **probris in hostem, reverentia adversus senes.**

Several verbs of external action take a genitive of the object akin to the above: as, **regno** Hor. *Od.* iii 30 12; **desino** ii 9 17, and sometimes **potior** (see **57**, and end of this case).

72. Objective Genitive of Thought and Feeling. Memini etc. The accusative is allowed with all verbs of memory, and with **recordor** is the usual construction. Other idioms: **Venit mihi Platonis in mentem** Cic. *Fin.* v 1 2: **fac tibi paternae legis Aciliae veniat in mentem** *i Verr.* 17 51. **Recordor** with persons takes **de.** Caesar uses **memini** to *mention* with the genitive (*b. c.* iii 108 2).

73. The Object of Feeling is in the genitive with verbs of pity except **miseror** and **commiseror. Nec studeat tui** Terence in Cic.

N. D. iii 72; and in comedy **cupere, fastidire** govern the genitive case Plaut. *Aul.* 243. **Testimonii veritus** Cic. *Att.* viii 4 1. To this or the above may belong Horace's **decipitur laborum** (if correct) *Od.* ii 13 38. **Poenitere, pudere** are sometimes personal: a thing is **poenitendum** and **pudendum** in Livy: who has **assuefaciebant militem minus poenitere** xxii 12 10. **Nihil quod poenitere possit** Cic. *Tusc.* v 28 81: and the same in Plaut. *Stich.* 51. Besides the perfect deponent impersonals **pertaesum est** etc. there are **me miseretur** in Cic. (**fratrum te misereatur** *pro Lig.* v 14) and **me veritum est** *de Fin.* ii 13 39. Ennius in Cic. *Or.* 46 155 says, **patris mei meum factum (factorum) pudet. Pudet deorum hominumque** *before gods and men* Liv. iii 19 7: similarly **pudor ipsius** Cic. *Fam.* v 1. (Compare perhaps the gen. with **interest** *there is concern in respect of him.*) With this genitive we may place that after interjections **heu facti** and others.

There is an analogy with the gen. of crime (and merit?) above.

74. The Genitive with Adjectives. Some may be classified, but so many remain that a general heading like **Genitive of Relation** seems necessary: if so, some will drop out of the other classes. A few cases are noticeable.

(*a*) **Objective.** Sometimes this alone distinguishes an adjective from a participle: as, **avitae nobilitatis retinens: dignitatis retinens: sui negotii bene gerens** in Tacitus. Cicero uses **colens** and **fugiens** with the genitive: Virgil has **servantissimus aequi** *Aen.* ii 427: Cicero **adpetens (gloriae)** *de Imp.* 3 7: add **patiens iniuriae** Phaedrus v 3: **impotens** with or without **irae** *passionate.* **Capax** with gen. not before Livy: **formidolosiorem hostium** Tac. *Ann.* i 62: **tenax propositi** Hor. *Od.* iii 3 1.

(*b*) **Thought and feeling: imprudens laborum** Virg. *Geo.* ii 372: **certus eundi** *Aen.* iv 554: **certus relinquendae vitae** Tac. *Ann.* iv 34: **gnarus prudens militiae, peritus** and **consultus** genitive (but abl. older **iure peritior** Cic. *Clu.* 38 107): **fessi rerum** *toil-weary* Virg. *Aen.* i 178: **trepidae rerum** xii 589: **lasso maris** Hor. *Od.* ii 6 7: **laeta laborum** Virg. *Aen.* xi 73: perhaps **integer vitae** *blame-*

less Hor. *Od.* i 22: **eloquentiae praeclarus** Tac. *Ann.* iv 34: **notus animi paterni** Hor. *Od.* ii 2 6 (suggesting approval), but see below.

(*c*) **Fulness and association**: analogous to abstract genitive after words of quantity: **spei plenus** *hopeful* (or abl.). Its use with verbs is given under the Ablative of Association. Less obvious uses are perhaps **dives opum** Virg. *Aen.* i 161: **largus opum** xi 338: **purgatus morbi** Hor. *S.* ii 3 27: **vetus militiae** Tac. *H.* iv 20: **integer** and **maturus aevi** Virg. *Aen.* ix 255 and v 73: **modicus voluptatis, pecuniae, originis** Tac. *Ann.* vi 39: **rudis insuetus** and **suetus**: **insolens infamiae** Cic. *Att.* ii 21. To these may be added scattered fragments of a genitive of **possessor** after **par** and **sacer**, of **comparison** with **secundus**, a (sociative?) genitive with **proximus** and **propinquus** (**fluminis propinqua loca** Tac.), besides those in which **animi** occurs: **inops animi, anxius, atrox** (**crucior, miseratus** Virg. *Aen.* vi 332), **sanus mentis**, and in Liv.; **fati melior** Sil. v 333. If **animi** were locative we should expect to find other expressions of place with adjectives. **Grecisms** are also a resource: but Grecisms must be founded on some Latin basis: and such may perhaps be found in the genitive of **relation**, which is the widest significance of the case, and would include the genitives with verbs of fulness (association) and **potior**.

For **Genitive of Fulness** see under **Ablative Case sec. 38.**

ADJECTIVES

75. The **adjective in its qualifying use** is an attribute or predicate not of concrete nouns, but only of words of class, and relates to the qualities of that class, as, **bonus artifex, sceleratus civis, fur manifestus, urbs munitissima.** Qualities of individuals are expressed by a substitution: **Scipio vir fortissimus, ille tam bonus civis, ista tua minime avara coniunx** Cic. *Ph.* ii 44 113, or by such phrases as **melior consulum.** But any adjective may go with a name in a **defining** sense: as, **minor Africanus, Pompeius Magnus,** even **Magnus Alexander** Liv. viii 3 7. One noun with several defining words is singular in **legio Martia atque quarta** Cic. *Phil.* v 17 46, plural in **prima et vicensima legiones** Tac. *Ann.* i 31. Compare **P. et L. Scipiones** Liv., **T. et C. Gracchus** Sallust.

76. Other parts of speech are used attributively: as in Livy, **omnia circà, deinceps reges, caede invicem, his invicem sermonibus** ix 3 4: **sola super imago** Virg. *Aen.* iii 489: **obviam itio** Cic. *Att.* xi 16: **Etrusci ante signa omnes** Liv. ix 32 9: **simul Punico Romanoque bello** ix 19 13: **omisso ad castra itinere** ix 35 7: **visu inter se** Tac. *Ann.* iv 2: compare the use of cases with nouns under accusative and abl. case. The predicative dative in **-ui** is used as an attribute in Late Latin, **33.** Perhaps an imitation of the Greek use with the article.

77. Qualifying expressions are not so readily transferred from persons to things as in English: *e.g. a human voice* is **vox hominis,** *mourning attire* **insignia lugentium,** *a drunken peace* **pax inter temulentos** Tac. *Ann.* i 50: except in the simpler generalisations such as **audax, fidele, perditum consilium, sceleratae preces, causa inpudentissima, inpudens postulatio** Liv. xxi 20 4: **adroganti et subdolâ morâ** Tac. *Ann.* iii 7: **suspicacis silentii** iii 11: **diligens contemplatio** Cic. *N. D.* i 19 50: **superbas Tarquini fasces** Hor. *Od.* i 12 34: **inpudenti censu** Cic. *ad Br.* i 18 5, or with modification as **petulans quoddam genus dicendi** *an impudent tone*; *a wise plan* is **consilium plenum prudentiae.**

78. The following **adjectives are used either for qualifying or for defining. Summus** and **medius,** usually in agreement either in 'partitive' or in qualifying sense: as in **medius collis** or as in **mediam se locavit** Virg. *Aen.* i 698: they are also used with the genitive: **summa** (pl.) **collis** *the hill-top*: but **medio campi** *in the plain between.* **Omnis** *every kind of*: **poenas expendimus omnes** Virg. *Aen.* xi 258: **haec te omnis** (*universal*) **dominatio regnumque iudiciorum delectat** Cic. *i Verr.* 12 35: **omni morte tristior deditio** Liv. ix 6 3. **Alius** *other* and **alii** *the rest of*: **in alia omnia ire** *to vote dead against a motion* and **alia omnis multitudo.**

Elliptical use: **quid est aliud tollere ex vita vitae societatem?** (**quid est aliud quam hoc?**) Cic. *Phil.* ii 4 7. **Alius** *different*: as in **longè alius** and **tam alius**. With abl. of comparison: **aliud sapiente bonoque** Hor. *Ep.* i 16 20. **Alias** adverb in **nunquam alias, non alias** *never before.* **Ceteri** *all others*, with no nom. sing. masc.: **cetera iurisdictio** Cic. *Att.* vi 2 5: **cetera classis** Liv. xxxv 26 9.

79. Adjectives as Substantives. **Bonus** does not mean *a good man.* Some words have become completely substantives as **amicus, medicus, iuvenis, volucris, bonum, commodum** etc. All adjectives may be used alone in the masc. or neut. pl. of class entire or abstract, not of members of the class, and so can neither be qualified nor defined as a rule: *e.g.* we must say **multi Romanorum, boni homines permulti, multa et adversa**: except with special words: as, **sacra** *rites*, **hiberna** *winter-quarters*, **mandata** *instructions*, **mortales** *human beings in multitudes*, **multi alii** (noun) **urbani** Cic. *Att.* iv 18 3; and **omnia** *a scene of*, **nive oppleta, lubrica, infesta, paludosa omnia**; **plena omnia malleorum** (**sec. 69**). In **Quae utrobique pulcra meminerit** Tac. *Ann.* vi 37, **pulcra** is predicative. The 'partitive' genitives in such phrases as **paludosa litorum, strata viarum** are really abstract, as may be seen under that genitive. The gen. dat. and abl. plural of these neuters are rarely used: **sperat infestis** Hor. *Od.* ii 10 13: **pavidos adversis** Tac. *Ann.* ii 14: **promptus ferocibus** *id.*: **nihil abnuendo veniam omnium accepere** *id.*: **iuvenem facilem inanibus** *id.*: **gaudens Bellona cruentis** Hor. *S.* ii 3 223.

In the singular of class not of individuals, as **sapiens, avarus, cupidus** *the sage*, *the miser* etc.: **inconsiderati est** Cic. *Phil.* iii 5 12: and in Hor., **pinguem vitiis albumque nec ostrea Nec scarus... poterit iuvare** (*Sat.* ii 2 21). (Still Hor. has **abnormis sapiens** *an eccentric philosopher*, *Sat.* ii 2 3.) Oftenest in oblique cases.

The neuter singular, properly 'partitive' (**nihil veri**) is extended through the influence of Greek: **alieni adpetens** Sall. *Cat.* 5: **inter silvas Academi quaerere verum** Hor. *Ep.* ii 2 45. It is rarely defined: as, **eo nefario** Liv. ix 34 19.

80. Adjective etc. as predicate or in apposition. When the subject expresses something without life or regarded as such, the predicate may be neuter: as, **triste lupus stabulis, dulce salix pecori** Virg. *Ec.* 3 80, 82. This is the rule with several subjects of different genders: **inimica sunt civitas et rex** (*i.e.* monarchy). Tacitus uses the neuter plural even with persons and in apposition: **parentes liberos fratres vilia** *Hist.* v 5. On the other hand persons and things regarded as persons have a masculine predicate when the genders differ: as, **Latium Capuaque agro multati** Liv. viii 11 13: **rex et regia classis una profecti** xxi 50: or the gender goes by the nearest subject as **Missae cohortes et praefectus** Sall. *Jug.* 77: **visas faces ardoremque caeli** Cic. *Cat.* iii 8 18.

81. Adverbial use of Adjective and Substantive or Secondary Predicate. The commonest adjectives used with predicative sense are those of

(1) **mental states**: as, **laetus, libens** *gladly*, **prudens** *intentionally*, **imprudens** *unawares* (Coleridge, *I blessed them unaware*), **sciens** *knowingly*, **invitus** *unwillingly*.

(2) **time**: as **serus, primus, ultimus,** less commonly **vespertinus, hodiernus**: **nunc sera adsurgis** Virg. *Aen.* viii 94: **solvite vela citi** iv 574: **stare perdius atque pernox** Gell. ii 1 (**ibant obscuri solâ sub nocte** Virg. *Aen.* vi 140).

(3) **place**: **praesens medius absens** etc.

(4) **degree, order, number** and other pronominal ideas: **ne nimia (vitis) fundatur** Cic. *de Sen.* 15 52: **plurimus imbre descendit** Virg. *Ec.* 7 60: **agmina terni Diductis solvere choris** *in three companies* (**terni** for **trini**?) *Aen.* v 581: **Philotimus nullus venit** Cic. *Att.* xi 29 4. So **si quem** Virg. *Aen.* i 181: **ea** vi 100: **quo numine laeso** and others under **sec. 5.**

(5) **dress**: **nudus ara, sere nudus** Virg. *Geo.* i 299: **ut paludati exeant** Caes. *b. c.* i 6 6.

Such words may agree with any noun in the sentence: **mediam se locavit** Virg. *Aen.* i 698: **ea vox audita laborum Prima tulit finem, primamque loquentis ab ore Eripuit pater** vii 118: **hostes imprudentes aggrediuntur** Caes. *b. c.* ii 38 4.

82. Any adjective or **class noun** may be considered adverbial when it qualifies the sentence as well as the term: as in **secundo** or **adverso flumine** or **vento**: **senem in patriam revertentem unde puer profectus sum** Liv. xxx 30 10: **diversi discedunt** x 33 10: even a name if emphasised: **Hannibal peto pacem** xxx 30 29: or a participle **nec te rationis egentem...circumstetit anguis** Virg. *Aen.* viii 300.

When the qualified term is a **particular thing or person, res, vir, homo, puer, mulier** should be added to qualifying adjectives, as above. **Itaque homo mitissimus atque lenissimus** (*for all his clemency and gentleness*) **non dubitat vinculis mandare** Cic. *Cat.* iv 5 10 (**sec. 8**).

For emphasis an **analytical form** is used: as, **invitus feci ut L. Flamininum e senatu eicerem** Cic. *de Sen.* 12 42.

For the adverbial accusative of the adjective see **sec. 20.**

83. Comparative and Superlative. The comparative may signify either something more or something less than the positive: **doctrina non moderata nec mitis sed paullo asperior et durior** Cic. *pro Mur.* 29 60. On the other hand **longior** *a little tedious*: **tristior** *almost sad* of Venus *Aen.* i 228.

Senex is the subst. masc. of the adjective **senior.**

Two different degrees of a quality are rendered by two comparatives: **Quum alia bella fortius quam felicius gessissent** Liv. v 43 7. **Magis quam** and **potius quam** with two positives mean *rather than.*

Vel with the superlative means *the very greatest* (perhaps *the greatest*) *degree*: **quam** or **quantus** with or without **possum** *the greatest possible.*

For **plus,** and **minus** indeclinable see **sec. 43** and **84.**

For the Case with Comparatives and Superlatives see under **sec. 43.**

Tac. omits the comparative in **miseratio quam invidia augebatur** *Ann.* iii 17: **claris quam vetustis** iv 61: **pacem quam bellum probabam** i 58 (**octavo mense quam** Liv. xxi 15 3).

NUMERALS

84. **Unus** often adds emphasis: **iustissimus unus qui fuit in Teucris** Virg. *Aen.* ii 427: or expresses contempt: as, **unus adolescens** *a mere lad*, **unus gladiator nequissimus** *a wretched cut-throat* Cic. *Ph.* ii 3 7: **ad unius voluntatem** of a tyrant *Fam.* iv 7 3. **Unum ex omnibus, unum omnium** *one above all* or *different from all*: but **unum ex togatorum numero** *a mere unit*, *de Or.* i 25 112: **unus de multis** *one of many such*. **Mille** indecl. adj. is often a substantive in Livy.

Plus, minus, amplius with numbers are indeclinable (except **pluris** and **minoris**) and neuter, and form one expression with the numeral: as, **pluris unius assis** Hor. *S.* i 6 14: **plus quam iv milia effugerunt** Liv. xxxix 31 13. See further under **Comparatives**, and under **Abl. of Comparison sec. 43** for instances of Age.

Ordinals. **Unus et alter** *several*: **alter et alter** *a pair*: **alterum tantum (fenoris)** 100 *per cent.*: **alter ego, alter idem** *a second self*: **nec alterius** gen. of **neuter.** The ordinal is the divisor or denominator in a fraction: **quota pars** *how few* of a number: **quotus esse velis rescribe** *how many others you want with you*, Hor. *Ep.* i 5 30: see also **quisque sec. 97.**

85. **Distributives** are used for equal distribution (unequal by **quisque**): often with the preposition **in**: **treceni denarii in capita** or **in militem.** They are often used in pairs and always in the plural (except as an archaism as in **trinum nundinum** *the time between three nundinae*). 10 *each* is **deni singulos.** Sometimes the thing distributed is in the plural without a distributive, as **milibus** for **singulis milibus**: **universi selibras contulerunt** Liv. v 47 8: **libras et sextarios** vii 37 3: **bina iugera et semisses** vi 16 7: **terna iugera quadrantibus adiectis** viii 11 14.

Distributives are also used with adverbial numerals in multiplication. **Deciens** (with **centena milia** expressed or understood) is *a million sesterces*: **bis bini** *twice two* (**bis senos laetantes agmine**

cycnos Virg. *Aen.* i 393): without adverb **bini** stands for the numeral *two*, or *a pair.* Often in poets for **duo.**

Distributives (usually **uni, bini, trini**) also express a multiplier: as, **binae litterae, binos ludos, bina castra** meaning several collections of things. **Octonis Idibus** *on the Ides of eight different months,* Hor. *Sat.* i 6 75: **bina die siccant ovis ubera** Virg. *Ec.* 2 42: **terna** (for **trina**) **hiberna** *Aen.* i 266.

PRONOUNS

For agreement see **sec. 5.**

86. PERSONAL PRONOUNS. **Equidem** seems to be used by Cicero by a false analogy for **ego quidem.** **Ego** and **tu** often follow **ne** (see under **Adverbs**). Personal pronouns and **ille** emphasize a conjunction or a balancing word: **Nec dulces amores Sperne puer neque tu choreas** Hor. *Od.* i 9 16: **Nunc dextrâ ingeminans ictus nunc ille sinistrâ** Virg. *Aen.* v 457. **Tu** has didactic force. **Tu regibus alas Eripe** *your part is to pluck their wings, Geo.* iv 106.

87. REFLEXIVE PRONOUNS. **Se** and **suus** refer properly to the subject of the clause in its most limited sense: sometimes to another word in it: as, **desinant insidiari domi suae consuli** Cic. *Cat.* i 13 32: **domum clausam suâ obice** Liv. ix 2 10: **insignia sua consulibus** ix 6 5: **suo sibi gladio hunc iugulo** (**sibi** to strengthen **suus**) Ter. *Ad.* v 8 35: **Arretinos in suâ possessione retinebam** Cic. *Att.* i 19 4. In a participial clause they may sometimes refer to the main sentence as in **dicitur (Papirius) Gallo barbam suam permulcenti iram movisse** Liv. v 41 9: **legationibus prae se ad senatum missis** ix 40 20: **non consulibus a se creatis exercitus tradiderunt** ix 20 1: very rarely to the general subject of discourse: as, **fuit hoc luctuosum suis** Cic. *de Or.* iii 2 7: **quo puer ipse modo, secum quo Troia pubes** Virg. *Aen.* v 599: **boves militibus dedit qui secum fuerant** Liv. vii 37 3. With thought or speech expressed or implied they refer to the person thinking or speaking: as, **misit qui vocarent ad**

se: rarely even in an inserted indicative clause: as, **hunc sibi ex animo scrupulum, qui se..stimulat, ut evellatis postulat** Cic. *Rosc. Am.* ii 6. In indirect speech **is** is used by Sulpicius in *ad Fam.* iv 20: so, **quo saepe ipsi maioresque eorum venissent** Liv. ix 5 9. **Suus** refers to persons not expressly mentioned in **iam Romae etiam sua infamis clades erat** Liv. ix 7 6. Compare **sec. 96, 182.**

After **suus, quisque** and **ipse** are regularly in apposition with the possessor; but are also used in the genitive (**suum ipsius** etc.): **divisum in suas cuiusque clientelas** Caes. *b. g.* vii 32 5: or agreeing with the thing possessed; **suismet ipsis praesidiis** Liv. viii 25 6; **suae cuique genti** xxv 17 5.

88. RECIPROCAL PRONOUNS. For want of a Middle Voice these must be expressed by phrases as **inter se. Invicem** is first used in Livy. Other expressions are **alter alterum, modo huc modo illuc**: but see under **Middle Voice, sec. 100.**

89. DEMONSTRATIVES. When the relative or its adverbs follow the main sentences they are usually balanced by **is** and its adverbs **eo, ita, tum, tamen** etc. Sometimes, however, the balance is made by a verb: as, **misit qui, praemium proposuit qui.**

Ille..qui means *the particular man who.* **Phaselus ille, quem videtis** Catullus iv 1. **Ille** is often allusive or historical; *the famous one*, or, *he in the story*: **sic Iupiter ille monebat** *warned, you remember*, Virg. *Aen.* vii 110. **Ac velut ille...lupus** xi 809. **Boletus... quales Claudius edit Ante illum uxoris** Juv. v 147. It never means *that of*, which has no parallel in Latin. It is often complimentary: as, **Alexander ille** *the great.* In Indirect Speech it is often used for **iste** contemptuous: **illam obsidionem flagitii ratus** Tac. *Ann.* iii 20. **Caput autem litterarum sibi cum illâ mimâ posthac nihil futurum** Cic. *Phil.* ii 31 77. In a parenthesis it strengthens **quidem**: **neque obscurè illi quidem**: sometimes to balance a following **sed** Cic. *Phil.* i 6 17. **Ille aut ille** *so and so.* **Illud** of a new point raised: **sequitur illud, quod a Milonis inimicis saepissime dicetur** *I now come to an allegation which* etc. Cic. *pro Mil.* 5 12. **Simulque**

illud reputato *you have further to consider* Tac. **Sed haec vetera, illud vero recens, Caesarem meo consilio interfectum** Cic. *Phil.* ii 11 25. **Illud magis vereor, ne...**

Hic is used to balance when the relative clause precedes: as, **quem cepit vitrea fama, Hunc circumtonuit gaudens Bellona cruentis** Hor. *Sat.* ii 3 223. When it precedes (as often in Hor.) it has its full force: **haec quae commemoro sunt palam** Cic. *in Pis.* 5 11. **Hic** often means *modern*. **Hanc disciplinam** *modern education* opp. to **illam veterem** Cic. *ii Verr.* ii 3 7. **Hic** adverb *in Rome* and **haec** *life in Rome*. **Hunc hominem** modestly for *myself*: so **hic stilus haud petet ultro Quemquam animantem** Hor. *Sat.* ii 1 39. **His xxx diebus** becomes **illis** in indirect speech.

When **hic** and **ille** are used in contrast **hic** usually means *the nearer* or *latter*, **ille** *the farther* or *former*, but

Quocumque aspicias, nihil est nisi pontus et aer,
Fluctibus hic tumidus, nubibus ille minax.
Look where you will, nothing but sea and sky,
This swollen with wrack, that threatening with billows Ov. *Tr.* i 2 24.

Ipse (is-pse) means *the very same, self.* In old writers it is declined like **is** (**87**, **182**). **Reapse** (Plautus *Truc.* 815) for **re ea-pse.**

Idem adverbially means *and also*, **idemque** *and yet.* **Idem** denotes consistency underlying apparent contradiction, or else simple consistency: *in the same spirit.* **Atque idem ego compositionis auctor esse non destiti** Cic. *Phil.* ii 10 24. With dat. in poets.

90. THE RELATIVE. An antecedent following a relative is in the same case. **Sic tibi dent nymphae quae levet unda sitim**: rarely for emphasis it precedes in the same case: **urbem quam statuo vestra est** Virg. *Aen.* i 573: **eunuchum quem dedisti nobis quas turbas dedit** Ter. *Eun.* iv 3 11: **arma quae missuri eratis, iis censeo armetis milites** Pompey in Cic. *Att.* viii 12 A. 4.

Apparent attraction is often due to ellipsis: **eius generis cuius [quasdam] suprà demonstravimus** Caes. *b. g.* v 2 2: **notante iudice**

quo nosti populo Hor. *Sat.* i 6 15, *i.e.* **quo notante**: **venit [cum eis] cum quibus ante dictum est copiis** Liv. xxv 32 10: **non cui simulabat [se consulère] consulendo** iii 41 4. A relative recurring in another case after a conjunction is replaced by a personal or demonstrative pronoun expressed or understood: **quae quoniam rerum naturam sola gubernas, nec sine te** etc. Lucr. i 22: or **qui** is repeated without a conjunction. **Et qui** mostly *and he who.* Or the second relative is omitted: **quorum saevitiam non bona exsatient, placari nequeant** Liv. ix 1 9. Or noun instead: **ferret hiems** *Geo.* i 321. The relative may refer to an implied antecedent: as, **illa furia qui** Cic. *ad Fam.* i 9 15: **duo importuna prodigia...quos** with words between *pro Sest.* 17 38. For **uter** see below.

The three kinds of **Relative Clause** are dealt with under **sec. 183** etc.

91. INTERROGATIVES. **Quis** is used for **uter** in poetry: **quos igitur anteferret** Tac. *Ann.* i 47: **quem damnet labor aut quo vergat pondere letum** of Aeneas and Turnus Virg. *Aen.* xii 727: **quis iustius induit arma** (Pompey or Caesar) Lucan i 126: **quis nemori imperitet** *of two bulls*, Virg. *Aen.* xii 719. **Quid** is often used rhetorically like an adverb, meaning *pray* or *again*: as, **stulte Aquinates: quid? Anagnini?** Cic. *Phil.* ii 41 106: **quid quod** *once more*: **quid? quod obrogatur legibus Caesaris** i 9 23. **Uterne** doubtful in *ii Verr.* iii 83 191, but **utrumne** in Hor. *S.* ii 3 251: **quone** *ib.* 295 and **quantane** 317: **ecquandone** MSS. in Cic. *Fin.* v 22 63.

Uter is also a relative: **uter aedilis fueritve praetor, is...intestabilis esto** Hor. *S.* ii 3 181: **agnum hinc uter est pinguior...sume** Plaut. *Aul.* 327: **ei molesta erunt, in utro culpa erit** Cic. *Att.* i 11 1. Also indefinite: **si uter volet** legal expression *ii Verr.* iii 14 35 *if either of the two.*

92. DOUBLE FORMS of **quis** interrogative or indefinite and its compounds. **Quis, qua** indefinite and **quid** are properly substantival, **qui, quae, quod** adjectival: thus we have **qui homo? si**

quid boni, si quod bellum and **qui vir optimus esset** Liv. xxix 14 6. **Quisquam** subst. corresponds with **ullus, quisquis** with **quicumque.** But with nouns of class we have **civis quisquam, pictor aliquis** (or **nemo**) the substantive really qualifying the pronoun. **Qui** interr. and indef. and **aliqui** mean *sort of* and are rarer and more emphatic: **aliquae** fem. is archaic, **aliquae** plural not used. **Si qui** and **ne qui** on the other hand are found without substantive in Cicero; **si quae, ne quae** in both uses as well as **qua**: but never the simple **qua.**

93. UNIVERSAL RELATIVE (English *-ever*). **Quisquis, quicumque, quotquot** (cp. **quot** in **quotannis**), **qualiscumque** sometimes lose their relative force. **Liberos suos quibusquibus Romanis mancipio dabant** Liv. xli 8 10: **quoquo versus** *each way* Cic. *Phil.* ix 7 15: **Tu mihi quodcunque hoc regni concilias** *this little realm* Virg. *Aen.* i 78: **sin qualemcumque locum sequimur** Cic. *Fam.* iv 8: **censendo quodcumque** *by the mere fact of speaking to the motion* Liv. iii 40 7.

Quisquis, quicumque, qualiscumque may have a disparaging sense (Fr. *quelconque*) as above and in Lucr. **hoc aevi quodcumque est** Lucr. ii 16. **Quisquis** for **uter uter**: **quidquid levius meliusve putaris** Juv. x 344. **Quidquid** for **quidque** is common in Lucr. **Ut quidquid** in Cic. *Clu.* 19 52, **in suo quisquis gradu** Liv. viii 38 11 are doubtful readings (**sec.** 97).

94. INDEFINITE PRONOUNS. **Dixerit quis** or **quispiam** or **aliquis, dicet aliquis** *some one may say.* **Simplicior quis et est** (si implied) Hor. *S.* i 3 63: **unde minime quis crederet: haud facile quis dispexerit. Quae quis apud superos...distulit piacula** *Aen.* vi 568: **quantum quis damni professus erat** Tac. *Ann.* ii 26: **Cyzicum aut aliud quid sequemur** Cic. *Att.* iii 16 1: **alienum esse a sapiente non modo iniuriam cui facere verum etiam nocere** *de Fin.* iii 21 71. Tac. uses **ut quis** for **ut quisque** commonly. **Cum quid venti motum esset** Liv. v 48 2. **Aliquis** should never be translated *any one.* It often means *some one, some little*: **aliquâ in re** *on some one occasion*: **si tamen e nobis aliquid nisi nomen et umbra Restat** Ov. *Am.* iii 9 59. **Cavebat (Pompeius) magis quam timebat omnia, ne**

aliquid vos timeretis Cic. *pro Mil.* 24 66: **si aliquid remisisset** *if only a little.* **Das aliquid famae** Hor. *Sat.* ii 2 42 *if not much.* With irony and emphasis it stands for *somebody.* **Sunt aliquid manes** Prop. iv 7 1: **Si vis esse aliquid** Juv. i 74: **Fac ut me aliquem esse velis** Cic. *Att.* iii 15: **Aliquid facerem ut non facerem** *I'd give something not to do it* Ter. *And.* i 5 24.

Aliquis, the reverse of **quisquam,** is used negatively when the positive is suggested. **Indignamur quod nobis hoc primum acciderit nec alicui unquam usu evenerit** *i.e. we expected some instance* Cic. *Inv.* ii 54 104. **Nemo vir magnus sine aliquo adflatu divino unquam fuit** *without some at least* Cic. *N. D.* ii 66 166 (*without any* is **sine omni** rarely **sine ullo**). **Aliquis** may suggest **alius quis: Filius anne aliquis magnâ de stirpe nepotum** Virg. *Aen.* vi 864. **Ne iis quidem annis aliquid quam iram meditatum** MSS. and Orelli for **aliud quam** in Tac. *Ann.* i 4 but see **83** end.

95. Quispiam *some one or other* is rarer than **aliquis: quaeret quispiam = dicet aliquis.**

Quidam with consciously metaphorical expressions *a kind of*: **lux quaedam videbatur oblata** Cic. *Phil.* i 2 3: not usually translated. **Saltatori motus non quivis sed certe quidam est datus** *de Fin.* 7 24. Add **Est qui, sunt qui** with indicative of particular persons. **Sunt quos iuvat** Hor. *Od.* i 1 4.

Quisquam and **ullus** (**usquam, unquam**) are regularly used only after a negative or in a phrase virtually negative: as, **vix quisquam: rarò unquam: et quisquam numen Iunonis adorat Praeterea?** Virg. *Aen.* i 48: **non adeo has exosa manus victoria fugit Ut tantâ quicquam pro spe tentare recusem** xi 437: **prius enim rem transegit quam quisquam eum id facturum suspicaretur** Cic. *Phil.* ii 9 21. A negative is suggested in **taetrior tyrannus quam quisquam superiorum** *ii Verr.* iv 55 123: **quamdiu quisquam erit qui te defendere audeat, vives**; *no longer*, *Cat.* i 2 6: or by a condition; **aut nemo aut si quisquam ille sapiens fuit** *de Am.* 2 9: **erat enim, si cuiusquam, certè tuum** *de Fin.* iii 3 10: but there is no such suggestion in **aeque atque ullam aliam** *any other whatsoever*, *Ep. ad Brut.*

i 6 2: and there is an old reading **ceterae ullâ dignitate** in *Att.* vii 14 3 (Ernesti) which seems a better sense than the MSS. **illâ.**

Nonnulli *a few* or *many* is an instance of **Litotes, sec. 231.**

With **unus: nec quisquam alterius gentis unus tantum eâ arte** [**excellit**] Liv. xxviii 37 6.

96. DISTRIBUTIVE PRONOUNS. The adjectives **singuli** etc. are used for mere division (see below); **quisque** discriminates. It is rarely used without further definition, as, **census cuiusque** Liv. vi 27 6: **pro cuiusque merito** viii 12 1: **pro ingenio quisque** ix 3 1: but commonly follows **se** or **suus** as in **suum cuique tribuito.** Sometimes, apparently to avoid awkwardness, **suus** and **quisque** agree with the same word: **frumentum omne quîque** (abl.) **suo genere** Lucr. ii 371: **proclivitas ad suum quodque genus** Cic. *Tusc.* iv 12 28 (see end of **87** above).

For **quisque** in apposition see **sec. 6** (collective nouns).

97. With relative pronouns or particles **quisque** distributes the action of the verb: **ut quisque me viderat, narrabat** Cic. *i Verr.* 7 19: **in quo quisque genere excelleret** *de Or.* i 28 130. With ordinal numerals: **decimus quisque** *one in ten*: **primo quoque tempore** *as soon as may be*: so with **quotus** *what in order* (*what denominator*)? **quotus quisque** *what fraction, how few?* **quotus quisque reliquus** *how small a remnant* Tac. *Ann.* i 3 7. With superlatives in the singular **quisque** signifies a selected class: **boni** *the good*, **optimus quisque** *the good among a crowd of others.* When the plural number is used it refers to a number of groups: **fortissima quaeque consilia** *the boldest methods* (or *sets of plans*): **in optimis quibusque honoris certamen** *among the best societies* Cic. *de Am.* 10 34. From Pliny onwards the plural is the regular use. In old Latin **quisque** means *whoever, any, every*: **cuiusque populi cives vicissent, is alteri populo imperitaret** quoted in Livy from a document in i 24 3: so **quandoque** for **quandocumque** Tac. *Ann.* i 6, Hor. *Od.* iv 1 17. **Quisquis** on the other hand for **quisque** in Liv. viii 38 11 (dub.) and in Lucr. (end of **93**).

Uterque agrees with a noun distributed but takes a pronoun in the genitive: as, **uterque consul** but **uterque horum**. It is rarely used with a plural verb, as in Caes. *b. c.* iii 30 3 **uterque eorum... educunt** (Riem.).

THE VERB

VOICES

98. The Latin passive differs from the English in throwing the emphasis on the fact rather than on the person. This is especially the case with the infinitive, so that we often find such expressions as **Linqui pollutum hospitium et dare classibus austros** Virg. *Aen.* iii 61. The impersonal passive expresses this emphasis most fully: as, **sic itur ad astra** *this is the way to heaven* Virg. *Aen.* ix 641 : **eo perventum est** *so low are we fallen* : **concurritur** *the armies clash.* A special use is to express the act of a crowd. **Itur ad Atriden** Juv. iv 65 : **Concurritur** Hor. *Sat.* i 1 8: **Conclamatum ad arma** Liv. vi 28 3.

Intransitive verbs are occasionally used personally in the passive as **credo** Ovid *Fast.* iii 351; especially in the participle as **regnatus, triumphatus** in Hor.

99. The same Voices are kept together: a passive impersonal (including **potest** impersonal) has a passive infinitive after it: as, **coeptum est obsideri oppidum:** but **coepit** is used with **esse** and **fieri. Potest** and **coepit** may be used alone: **eo, si potest, acrius te rogo** Cic. *Att.* ii 24. Other instances, **sec. 132.**

100. The Middle Voice, probably the origin of the passive, is not a Grecism, but exists throughout Latin: **pascuntur silvas** Virg. *Geo.* iii 314, **rumperis irâ** Hor. *Sat.* i 3 136, **implentur** Virg. *Aen.* i 215, **circumfundimur** ii 383, **linquitur** *he faints*, **advehor** *I put in*, **vehor** *to drive in a carriage*, and its various compounds in the sense of *sailing.* **Vehor** and **lavor** have present participles in a middle sense: so **obversantem** Liv. xxxiv 61 4: **vertenti fortunae**

ix 17 6: **avertens** of Venus Virg. *Aen.* i 402. **Potior** is from **potire** *put in possession.* In the sense of *getting done* are **liceor** *bid* from **liceo** *put to auction*: **pignerari** *pledge* (**alveolos pignerat Atreus** *brings to the hammer* Juv. vii 73). In poetry the verbs and participles of clothing especially appear to be middle, as **exuor, indutus** etc., and govern the accusative case, **sec. 16.** Other instances are **expleri mentem nequit** Virg. *Aen.* i 713: **expedior** ii 633: **velare comas** iii 405 (imperat.): **abscissa vestes** iv 590: **accingendum** Liv. vi 35 2: **curati cibo** ix 37 7.

The reciprocal middle is expressed by **inter se, invicem** (late), **alter alterum** etc.: **vir virum legit: ultro citroque fide datâ** *with mutual assurances* Liv. xxix 23 5: **audire et reddere voces** Virg. *Aen.* i 409: **pedibus per mutua nexis** vii 66: **alterni innixi sublevantesque invicem** Liv. v 47 2.

The active has sometimes a middle sense in poetry: **prora avertit** Virg. *Aen.* i 104: **nox humida caelo Praecipitat** ii 9: rarely in prose; **animi mutaverant** Liv. ix 12 3: **flexit** Tac. *Ann.* i 13: **obstrinxit** i 14, iv 31.

TENSES

101. Tenses denote Time and State in the Indicative and in Oratio Obliqua. There are three simple times and three simple states of an action.

Present	aorist	*I loose*	**solvo**[2]	λύω[2]	je lâche
Past	aorist	*I loosed*	**solvi**[2]	ἔλυσα	je lâchai, j'ai lâché (familiar)
Future	aorist	*I shall loose*[1]	**solvam**	λύσω	je lâcherai[3]
Present	imperfect	*I am loosing*[1]	**solvo**	λύω	je lâche[2]
Past	imperfect	*I was loosing*[1]	**solvebam**	ἔλυον	je lâchais
Future	imperfect	*I shall be loosing*[1]	**solvam**[2]	λύσω	je lâcherai[2 3]
Present	perfect	*I have loosed*[1]	**solvi**	λέλυκα	j'ai lâché[1]
Past	perfect	*I had loosed*[1]	**solveram**	ἐλελύκη	j'avais lâché[1]
Future	perfect	*I shall have loosed*[1]	**solvero**	(in passive)	j'aurai lâché[1]

[1] analytical. [2] once analytical, now synthetic. [3] borrowed.

102. These nine tenses however do not exhaust the capabilities of tense: *e.g.* perfect may mean previous or complete: imperfect may mean begun, frequent, intended, or potential. Aorist is really a negation of state and may refer to single or sudden acts.

103. Tenses in other Moods. The *imperative* has no tenses: what is called the future is an old form used in legal formulas. The *infinitive* (apart from oratio obliqua) has only two forms to express all times and states. The *conjunctive* usually has no indication of time[1], but expresses by its four forms (1) the reflected time of the main sentence (sequence), (2) the distinction of state and act, (3) that of abstract and unreal. In case of difficulty, either (1) or (3) must be disregarded. Thus its four tenses denote

state	abstract *or* reflecting pres. or fut.	**solvam**
state	unreal *or* reflecting past time	**solverem**
act	abstract *or* reflecting pres. or fut.	**solverim**
act	unreal *or* reflecting past time	**solvissem**

The distinction of abstract and unreal may also be traced in the indicative tenses as will be seen below.

104. THE PRESENT TENSE besides its present meaning expresses a general fact, a state continuing from the past, a vivid past, and a contemplated future.

(*a*) **General fact or tendency: Sic itur ad astra** Virg. *Aen.* ix 641: **aditur (villa) non unâ viâ: libros capit** *can hold books*: **datur hora quieti** *Aen.* v 844: **sententia quae amicos parat** Liv. ix 3 12. The corresponding imperfect conjunctive appears in oratio obliqua: **quae ab se postea minore periculo necaretur** Cic. *Clu.* 15 45 (‘*can be killed’ she thought*). The ‘potential’ **longum est** *it would take long* literally means *it is a long task.* So **Possum Ni refugis** *I could* Virg. *Geo.* i 176.

[1] When it has, difficulties of sequence arise, which will be dealt with below.

The perfect Conj. is occasionally used of previous time in wishes and suggestions, but is more often abstract without time.

The perf. Conj. except in early Latin is identical with the fut. perf. Indic. both in forms and in varieties of quantity except in the first person singular. In some of its uses, as **dixerit aliquis,** it resembles the future Indicative.

[This idiom occurs in all the present and past tenses: in the imp. and plup. the stress is on the unreality: see below.]

(*b*) **State continuing**: sometimes with **iamdudum** *this long while*, **cupio iampridem Alexandream visere** Cic. *Att.* ii 5: **postquam** *ever since*, **postquam nos Amaryllis habet** Virg. *Ec.* 1 31: **sumus ante** *Aen.* i 98.

(*c*) **Vivid past**, of an act supposed to take place before the reader's eyes. This includes the Historic present, but there are other forms.

In descriptions of place, objects are supposed to be arranging themselves before the eye (*this river comes me cranking in*, Shakespeare 1 *H. IV* 3 1 99). **Insula portum efficit** Virg. *Aen.* i 159: **Urbs dividitur amni** Liv. xxv 17 10.

The Historic Present lays stress on past facts as such apart from their context, and in narrative is seldom continuous or dependent on other verbs: as, **Persius exponit causam: solem Asiae Brutum appellat** etc. Hor. *Sat.* i 7 22. The Hist. Present probably explains the present ind. with **dum** *while*, **sec. 202**, and **quum, sec. 200.**

105. A special form of the Historic Present is used in quotation, both in giving the authority and in relating the matter: **Homerus ait: inquit** etc. commonly, and **quod scribis** in letters: **liber qui inscribitur Menon** Cic. *Tusc.* i 24 57: again **Peleus raptum cum luget Achillem** Juv. x 256: so in appeals to memory or other records: **Cratera quem dat Sidonia Dido** Virg. *Aen.* ix 266: **quantum mutatus ab illo Hectore qui redit** ii 274: **creat** *Geo.* i 279: **generat** *Aen.* viii 141: **dat** ix 216: **mactas** *Ec.* 8 294: **edunt** *ib.* 45: **oneras** *Aen.* iv 549. [The same tendency appears in the conjunctive **sineret dolor** for **si sivisset** *Aen.* vi 31: **si Vergilio deesset Hospitium, caderent...hydri** Juv. vii 69: **dictis Albane maneres** *Aen.* viii 643 *you should have kept your word.*]

106. (*d*) **A Contemplated (not intended) future result. Produntur ea omnia deleto hoc exercitu non servantur**

Liv. ix 4 12: this is more common in the infinitive: **patriâ pelli Romanos** xxi 53 4: **aequari summa infimis** ii 9 3: **priori se consilio firmare pacem** ix 3 2: **rumpi non sperat amores** Virg. *Aen.* iv 292: **nequidquam defendi** Liv. ix 22 11.

In a **question** future time is often suggested by the present. This use differs from the deliberative conjunctive by merely asking the fact. **Imus in adversos** *are we to close?* **Quin conscendimus equos? Quid ago?** *Aen.* x 78: **An festinamus cum Germanici cineribus adpellere?** Tac. *Ann.* ii 77: **Quid censes? Conciditur?** *Do we cut it up?* Juv. iv 130: **in quâ te quaero proseuchâ** iii 296: **Romamne venio** (*do I come?* your decision not mine) **an Arpinum fugiam?** Cic. *Att.* xvi 8 2.

107. So in **conditions**, of the fact rather than the intention: **ni propere fit...iubebo** Liv. xxxvi 28 6: **si diem proferimus et...desierimus, periculum est** xxv 38 20: **si paret** *if it appears*; legal formula: **si non redditur** *if it is not to be replaced* Cic. *Phil.* i 7.17: **sic ignovisse me putato si cenas hodie mecum** (you may or may not) Hor. *Ep.* i 7 70.

In the **first person** the stress is on the fact rather than on the intention: **Sed ea non muto, non moveo** Cic. *Ph.* i 7 17: **describo et remitto** *Att.* ii 20 6: in the infinitive passive where the first person is meant: **responsum non recipi reges** Liv. ii 15 2: **se in auctoritate Tarentinorum manere nec descendere in aciem** ix 4 7: equivalent often to a **threat,** as in French: *dis, ou je t'assomme.*

So with **antequam** and **dum** *while* or *until.* **Ante, Pudor, quam te violo** Virg. *Aen.* iv 27: **dum breviter respondeo, quaeso ut audiatis** Cic. *Clu.* 4 8: **nec me meminisse pigebit Elissae Dum spiritus hos regit artus** Virg. *Aen.* iv 335: **dum eximus opperibere** Ter. *Haut.* iv 7 5: **si forte abesse dum patratur malles** Liv. xxiii 8 10: **antequam discedis** of the intention of another Cic. *Att.* xii 37 2 (see **Temporal Clauses, 202**).

108. THE IMPERFECT TENSE denotes:

(*a*) **A past habit** or series of acts. **Ille meum comitatus iter ...pelagique minas caelique ferebat** Virg. *Aen.* vi 113. The historic infinitive often takes its place, as, **neque Hasdrubal alium praeficere malle,** as well as **princeps in proelium ibat** in Hannibal's character Liv. xxi 4 8: but characteristic habit is aorist: **quales (boletos) Claudius edit** (to distinguish the kind of mushroom) Juv. v 147: **domum servavit, lanam fecit** epitaph on Cornelia quoted by Mommsen.

(*b*) Past state or act going on: **summis Amasenus abundans spumabat ripis** *was foaming* at the time Virg. *Aen.* xi 548. **Ibant obscuri solâ sub nocte per umbram** vi 268. Historic infinitive Tac. *Ann.* ii 23 etc. and **sec. 135**. A state may be described under the form of an act going on though really finished, as, **oppidum loci naturâ muniebatur** Caes. *b. g.* i 38 4.

(*c*) With **iamdudum** of a state continued from a further past: **iamdudum flebam** *I had been weeping* for a long time and *was still weeping* Ovid *Met.* iii 656.

109. (*d*) An incomplete past: **Trudebantur in paludem nisi Caesar legiones instruxisset** Tac. *Ann.* i 63: **iam tuta tenebam, Ni**—*I had reached safety, had not*—*Aen.* vi 358. **Vincebat, ni circummissus Veiens evasisset** Liv. ii 50 10 (see Conditional Clause **220**). The 'potential' imperfects **laurus erat, ni alium iactaret odorem** Virg. *Geo.* ii 133, **tempus erat** Hor. *Od.* i 37 4, **poteras** Virg. *Ec.* 1 79, **melius erat = esset**, all of present time, have a sense of unreality due to the tense, but practically the same as that of the past conjunctive. Comp. **sec. 220.**

(*e*) A past effect anticipated: **Milone interfecto haec assequebatur = assecuturus erat** Cic. *pro Mil.* xii 32. **At eo repugnante fiebat** (*expected to be elected*) xiii 34. **Num dubitas id me imperante facere quod iam tuâ sponte faciebas?** *Cat.* i 5 13. **Ita fratrem exheredans faciebat te heredem?** *Phil.* ii 16 41 *was he likely?*

(*f*) A past effort, attempt or intention. **Orabat** Virg. *Aen.* xi 535 and often: **mandata dabat** vi 116: **lenibat dictis animum** vi 468: **haec ut sciret quid non faciebat?** *Ec.* 2 35.

110. (*g*) A past act implied in another, which is given itself as a fact: **Censendo quodcumque, magistratus esse qui**

senatum haberent, iudicabat *by merely voting he implied the opinion that the president must be a magistrate* Liv. iii 40 7. **Qui nimios optabat honores numerosa parabat tabulata** *was thereby erecting a platform of many stories* Juv. x 104, **sec. 176.**

The above in the infinitive become aorist, except sometimes with **memini. Memini quae plagosum mihi parvo Orbilium dictare** Hor. *Ep.* ii 1 70 (**176**).

111. The **Epistolary Imperfect** (or aorist) is used when something present to the writer will be past when the letter is received: as for instance the date: **dabam** or **dedi**: not of permanent conditions or the relations between the correspondents: as, **ut spero, amabo te, hortor te, litteras tuas exspecto:** unless an exact time is referred to. The same holds for the perfect and pluperfect. **Nunc, adhuc, hodie** are not changed, although otherwise Cicero does not use **adhuc** for past time. Pliny the younger uses more freedom about the epistolary tense generally.

112. THE PERFECT TENSE. Logically there are **two tenses, a past-aorist** (*he did*) **and a present-perfect** (*he has done*): but we must guard against a refinement which was never completely realised: some idioms are only intelligible by forgetting the difference.

(*a*) **Among aorist uses** note one in which past states, habits and tendencies are regarded simply as facts (see under **Imperfect Tense 108**). **Lanam fecit** epitaph on Cornelia: **quales Claudius edit** Juv. v 147 of a type of mushroom: **quoad vixit credidit** Hor. *S.* ii 3 92. A bare **abstract fact** in the perfect indicative may from the nature of the verb express a duty or possibility, as in the present tense: **potuerunt haec fieri** (frequently): **melius fuit** of something which did not happen: after **ut** consecutive **ut melius fuerit non capi Veios** Liv. v 30 6: **quem metui** *whom had I to fear* Virg. *Aen.* iv 603: see further under **Vivid Sequence, sec. 122** D, and compare **sec. 206, 219.**

113. (*b*) **The true perfect** (perfect with 'have') expresses something done as bearing on **present** time, and is not a past tense. Particular cases are:

(1) **What has happened apart from time,** often, seldom, or never: **illius immensae ruperunt horrea messes** Virg. *Geo.* i 49: **multi multos amicos perdiderunt** Cic. *Fin.* i 15 49: **illum non purpura regum Flexit** Virg. *Geo.* iii 496. Often of the former of two frequent acts, with **quum** etc.: **quocumque aspexisti, ut furiae sic tuae tibi occurrunt iniuriae** Cic. *Parad.* 2.

(2) To express **a completed act in present time. Catilinam ex urbe eiecimus** Cic. *Cat.* i 1 1: with emphasis in **habeo scriptum** etc. This is the origin of the French form of the perfect and other tenses. Compare **sec. 115** (*b*).

(3) **Of an act completed in imagination. Periimus: actum est de republicâ** etc. **Sin funditus occidimus...fuero** Cic. *Q. f.* i 2.

(4) With completeness there may be **suddenness. Terra tremit, fugere ferae** Virg. *Geo.* i 330: **abiit, excessit, evasit, erupit** Cic. *Cat.* ii 1.

(5) **Of a state now ended or ending. Vixerunt** *they are no more*: **vixi et quem dederat cursum fortuna peregi** Virg. *Aen.* iv 654: **fuit Ilium** ii 325: and in a wish **Hac Troiana tenus fuerit fortuna secuta** vi 62. The form with **fui** is common in this sense. **Restituat legiones quo saeptae fuerunt** Liv. ix 11 3.

(6) A name is wanted for the vivid pluperfect signified in **Conticuere omnes intentique ora tenebant** *Aen.* ii 1, **Prosiluere** *they are off* v 139, which should be called Historic perfect had not that name been already adopted for the past aorist (**venit** *he came*).

Of these, (2), (4) and (6) are the common uses in Virgil.

114. THE PLUPERFECT TENSE denotes

(*a*) a past fact **preceding another** whether in the same sentence or not; as in **quum haec fecisset abiit: nec satis id fuerat, stultus quoque carmina feci** Ovid *ex Ponto* iii 3 37. **Provida Pompeio dederat Campania febres Optandas: sed multae urbes et publica vota Vicerunt** Juv. x 283.

When the other verb is imperfect, the pluperfect has a sense of **frequency**, which perhaps is due to the accompanying imperfect and not inherent in the tense: **cum rosam viderat, tum incipere ver arbitrabatur** Cic. *ii Verr.* v 10 27: **ut cuiusque sors exciderat, alacer arma raptim capiebat** Liv. xxi 42 3.

The subsequent act may be in a primary tense (as in **Vixi et quem dederat cursum fortuna peregi** above). **Si quando adepta est id quod concupitum fuerat** followed by present Cic. *Tusc.* iv 15 35. **Legerat...perferet** Juv. vii 152: **nunc certe promenda tibi sunt consilia: hoc fuerat extremum** *advise me; my wits are at an end* Cic. *Att.* ix 8 2: **est .. quum non fuisset** iv 16 1.

The subsequent act may be only implied, as in **Promissa parenti Discedens dederam** (and yet I broke it) Virg. *Aen.* xi 46.

115. (*b*) The pluperfect is used of **an action completed at some past time** which may be denoted by an imperfect: **dederatque comam diffundere ventis** Virg. *Aen.* i 319: **ter circum Iliacos raptaverat Hectora muros** followed by **vendebat** i 483. In periphrasis there is a greater sense of completeness: **deorum templis bellum semper habuit indictum** Cic. *ii Verr.* v 72 108.

Completeness may imply **suddenness**: **flammas quum regia puppis Extulerat** Virg. *Aen.* ii 257: **quo metu Italia omnis contremuerat** Sall. *Jug.* 114.

Or of **a state long ended.** **Si mihi, quae fuerat, si nunc foret illa iuventas** Virg. *Aen.* v 397: **non sum ego qui fueram** Prop. i 12 11.

Or of **an unreal past**; whether an act which nearly happened or a past duty or possibility unrealized. **Me truncus illapsus cerebro Sustulerat, nisi Faunus ictum Dextrâ levasset** Hor. *Od.* ii 17 28: **praeclare viceramus nisi Lepidus recepisset Antonium** Cic. *Fam.* xii 10. With these compare **debueram, melius fuerat,** as **Vivere debuerant et vir meus et tua coniunx** Ovid *F.* vi 591: **Aequius huic Turnum fuerat se opponere morti** Virg. *Aen.* xi 115: **Verum anceps pugnae fuerat fortuna** (*would have been*) iv 603.

The latter becomes **fuisset** after **ut: Ut nisi foedus esset memoria cessisset** Liv. ii 33 9. This and the corresponding imperfect use are perhaps traces of the 'unreal' meaning of past tenses more plainly to be seen in the Conjunctive.

The pluperfect form with **fuerat** when used with that with **erat** denotes the earlier of two acts: so with other forms **Se recordatum esse sibi tabernaculum captum fuisse** Cic. *N. D.* ii 4 11.

The form of the pluperfect with **forem** is not common till after Cicero.

116. FUTURE TENSE. This, even more than the present and perfect, expresses a general fact apart from time: as, **servis regna dabunt, captivis fata triumphos** Juv. vii 201. This may take the form of:

(*a*) **General fact**: **non tuus hoc capiet venter plus ac meus** Hor. *Sat.* i 1 46: **pueri ludentes 'rex eris,' aiunt 'si recte facies'** *Ep.* i 1 60.

(*b*) **Permission** or liberty to do a thing, *passing into* **command**: **cantabit vacuus coram latrone vĭator** *the bare tramp may whistle at the highwayman* Juv. x 22: **facies ut sciam** *you may let me know* (modest but absolute, cp. **ne feceris 128**): **scriberis Vario** *you may get Varius to record you* Hor. *Od.* i 6 1: **alternis dicetis** Virg. *Ec.* 3 59: **referes ergo** *Aen.* ii 547: **cantabitis** *Ec.* 10 31: *The guards will advance.*

(*c*) **Concession** (*may perhaps*): **laudabunt alii claram Rhodon** *let others praise bright Rhodos* Hor. *Od.* i 7 1: **excudent alii spirantia mollius aera** Virg. *Aen.* vi 847: **dicet aliquis** (**dicat** rare: Roby): **quaeres fortasse: invidia metuet** *Geo.* iii 38.

(*d*) **Indignation** as in Greek: **comitabor?** *Aen.* iv 547: **moriemur?** 659.

117. THE FUTURE PERFECT. This is commonly used to denote the **former of two future acts**; as, **Cum sol accenderit aestus In secreta senis ducam** Virg. *Geo.* iv 401. **Negaro: videbor** Cic. *Ph.* xi 8 19: **opportune ante venerit** *Att.* x 9 4.

Often of a **future act with reference to its effect**: **ut sementem feceris ita metes** Cic. *de Or.* ii 65 261: **si proprium hoc fuerit, de marmore stabis** Virg. *Ec.* 7 31.

Of what will be a **fact in future time**, though not necessarily a future event: *e.g.* **in indignant questions**: **Occiderit ferro Priamus** [*if Helen live*] Virg. *Aen.* ii 581. **Impune ergo mihi recitaverit ille togatas Hic elegos?** [*if I spare him*] Juv. i 3: **Ibit et...illuserit?** Virg. *Aen.* iv 591. So without a question often **with imperative**: **ite ad senatum;...potestatem habueritis** *you will find you have the powers* Liv. vi 26 2: **tu invita mulieres; ego accivero pueros** *you will find I have fetched the men* Cic. *Att.* v 1: **tolle hanc opinionem; luctum sustuleris** *Tusc.* i 13 30: **Clamet amica...non magis audierit** Hor. *S.* ii 3 60: **Te me dextera Defensum dabit...tu facito** Virg. *Aen.* xii 437. In relation to another future unexpressed: **sin plane occidimus, ego omnibus meis exitium fuero** *I shall prove to have been* Cic. *Q. f.* i 4: **ego videro, alias viderimus**: add **faxo** *I'll warrant*, which is future perfect at least in this use. In Conjunctive **ita ulciscar ut ne plane inluseris** Ter. *Eun.* iv 4 20. In comedy and letters this passes into a vivid future: **facile eum acceperint** Cic. *Att.* i 1 2: **valde videro** (Atticus *loq.*) ix 10 9: **quid historiae de nobis ad annos dc praedicarint?** ii 5 1.

118. The above **two uses taken together** signify a mutual or identical effect: **qui Antonium oppresserit is bellum confecerit** *will thereby finish the war* Cic. *Fam.* x 19. **Nihil maius praestiteris quam si hic dies documentum dederit** Liv. viii 35 7. **Pergratum feceris si disputaris** Cic. *de Am.* 4 16.

Very rarely the future perfect denotes a **state about to end.** **Brevis est hic fructus homullis; iam fuerit** Lucr. iii 926.

119. SEQUENCE OF TENSES. The rule is that in **Mental Clauses** in the Conjunctive the present tenses (including the perfect with '*have*') follow the present or future, and past tenses follow past either in the Mental Clause or in its governing verb. It must be borne in mind that both the present and the past

Indicative include acts and states in three aspects, as aorist, continuous, and complete. The difficulties in Latin are mainly two.

(*a*) In the inf. etc. the perfect may be **at the same time completed present and past-aorist**: as, **dico te venisse ut scires.** Cic. thus writes regularly **Quemadmodum officia ducerentur satis explicatum arbitror** *de Off.* i 43 152: **nunc...fugisse...ne adiret** Liv. xxi 63: **processit astrum...gauderent** Virg. *Ec.* 9 48: **vidi...quae eruerent** *Geo.* i 318. The same with the perfect conjunctive. **Requiescere putat...magnâ culpâ Pelopis qui non erudierit...quatenus esset** Cic. *Tusc.* i 44 107 (Riem.): **cogitare quid sim facturus, si acciderit** (perfect) **ut legarer** *Att.* x 1 4. Generally speaking the Conjunctive has no past Aorist: except in the consecutive clause, which in some ways resembles the indicative: **ut ne se quidem servare potuerit** (aor.) **quîn una rempublicam vosque servaret** Cic. *pro Mil.* xi 30.

120. (*b*) The other difficulty is the conflict between **past sequence and unreality**, both expressed by the same conjunctive tenses.

(1) An '**unreal**' conjunctive may regularly follow a present in the main sentence. **Quaero a te cur ego C. Cornelium non defenderem** Cic. *in Vat.* 2 5. **Video permultas causas esse quae istum impellerent** *pro Rosc. Am.* 33 92. A reason may be found in the words being the writer's own (**193**).

(2) An '**unreal**' conjunctive is **regularly followed** by an **imperfect** conjunctive though with present meaning. **Nisi apud quos haec haberetur oratio cernerem** (*is being spoken*) Cic. *de Or.* i 42 190: **cuperem vultum videre tuum quum legeres** *Att.* iv 17 4.

(3) But **not** if an '**unreal**' conjunctive is followed by an **abstract general** thought. **Si concederetur, etiam si ad corpus nihil referatur, ista per se esse iucunda** Cic. *de fin.* i 7 25. Nor when stress is laid on **fact**, as in **Quae acciderint quererentur** Liv. xxvi 31 8: **ut hoc diceret** (*should now say*) **se quanti voluerit vendidisse** Cic. *ii Verr.* ii 4 16. Or when present time is marked: **mallem** (=**malo**) **audire Cottam, dum...inducat** *N. D.* ii 1 2, yet see

cuperem (2) above: **haud ita conveniebat** (= **conveniret**) **ut videatur** Lucr. iii 682.

Anomalous instances occur. **Puto tibi venire in mentem** (imperf. inf.?) **quae vita esset nostra** Cic. *Att.* iii 20 1 (comp. the inf. with **memini sec. 110**): **scitote esse oppidum in Sicilia nullum... quo in oppido non...mulier delecta esset** *ii Verr.* v 11 28. Here the conj. follows the general sense which is historic. Or see **sec. 193.**

Early and colloquial Latin observe the sequence less. **Tabellas dedi cuidam cui deferat...ut veniret** Plaut. *Mil.* 131. **Si te flocci facio an periisses prius** *Trin.* 992.

121. (4) **The Vivid Sequence.** In reported speech the time of narrative may be disregarded and the present and perfect Conjunctive used either after a historic present, in quoting or forecasting fact, or appealing to the audience. See Note below.

NOTE ON THE VIVID SEQUENCE IN LIVY

122. This is often due to historic present as in the speeches of Manlius and Hannibal Liv. xv 7, xxi 30; but is common after a past sequence as throughout v 10 and vi 5. The historic present often has past sequence. Other causes are to be found in the relations of speaker and audience.

A. **Questions** asked and answered by the speaker or a third party with their dependent clauses follow historic sequence. **Quantopere optandum foret...Hernicos docuisse** Liv. ix 45 7. (For the exceptional **Mirari se quinam terror invaserit** see under E below.)

But **ad pacem inclinent animi falli non posse** means *you cannot doubt* (ix 45 3). **Sciat unusquisque** (after **ut**) **quid alieni sit** *you all know* vi 27 8.

B. A **command** is historic, an appeal primary. **Sperent** xxi 30 11 is perhaps for **speremus**, preceded as it is by the command **crederent**. (So perhaps the appeal of Vercingetorix in Caes. *b. g.* vii 64.) The **prayer** in vi 23 11 shared no doubt by the crowd present is primary, but the personal prayer v 21 15 is historic in sequence.

C. **Purpose** generally is historic, as **daturum se operam ne vellent** xxi 45 5: that of the audience is primary: **neque meritum neque iniuriam esse ob quae sumant arma** *why you should expect us to fight* xxi 20 5. A purpose implied in its fulfilment is primary: **bellum trahi ut gerant** (*you*) v 10 7: **ne quies sit** (*to you*) v 10 7: **omnia fieri ut consenescat exercitus** (*you* the army) v 11 9: so with **donec** vi 27 8.

D. A logical **consequence** (*so as to*) is historic: as, **nec quemquam esse qui vellet** xxi 53 2: **tunc cum effecerint ne quis perferret** vi 28 9: but consequence asserted as a fact (actual or hypothetical) is primary: **ne in turbâ quidem haerere quemquam qui admoneat** v 2 11: **ut habeat** (as a fact) v 11 4: **ut verisimilius sit** v 11 7: **ut melius fuerit** *so that you see it would have been* v 30 6: and in the periphrasis with **fuerit** and future participle (never **fuisset**).

E. Either facts or ideas **coming from the speaker** will be historic: **esse quod reficerent** *there is a reason for electing us again* vi 39 11: **quoniam scirent** (so the speaker argues) ix 4 3: **quibus acciperent animis gesturos** *we will carry it on in the same spirit as we receive it* xxi 18 14. This though 'regular' is by no means very common. But the **mind or knowledge of the audience** are appealed to in primary sequence: **quibus dilectus sit gravis** *you who feel the burden of conscription* v 11 5: **eos quos cernant legatos** xxi 30 7: **quae tum cecinerit** (a known fact) v 15 10: **quod quum quia** of known facts: **satis poenarum dedisse quod facti sint privati** v 11 12: **quum viderint** v 11 14: **fugere tabulas quia nolint** (*as you know*) vi 27 6: so **infeliciorem quam fuerit** vi 5 3: **quum liceat, non uti** v 11 16: **quum aggressus sit** (*whereas*) vi 11 5: **ita pugnaturos ut pugnaverint** vi 28 9: **quoad vires habuerint incursiones factas** vi 5 3: even in a question; as, **mirari se quinam terror...invaserit** xxi 30 2 after historic present.

Especially a **known general truth** is in primary sequence: **Gallos cum quibus nec bellum nec pax fida sit** v 17 8: **quum ita ferme eveniat** v 20 6: **postquam in conspectu Alpes habeant quorum alterum latus Italiae sit** xxi 30 5: **terrae eae quas duo maria amplectantur** *ib.* sec. 2: (the last two perhaps affected by the historic present).

F. A **condition** not yet fulfilled is historic: **si vellent** vi 39 11, and **qui vellet** v 20 4 of a choice offered. But a condition fulfilled though doubtful to the speaker is primary. **Si quid eorum displiceat, redire vetuit** *if you are dissatisfied now* ix 4 5: **si quis recte aestimari velit** (*i.e.* **si vultis**) vi 11 4: **si timeant (si timetis)** vi 28 6: **nec stricturum ante gladium, si per Gallos liceat (si per vos licet)** xxi 24 4: **injustè facere si praeponat** (*as you seem to do*) xxi 11 2.

G. A **promise** or **threat** takes historic sequence, but the **prospect** of a coming event is in primary sequence: as,

{**priusquam aqua emissa foret...non potiturum** (oracle v 15 4).
{**antequam id fiat, deos deserturos non esse** (*ib.* sec. 11).
{**ratum fore si populus censuisset** (law xxi 19 3).
{**gratius fore quod quisque rettulerit** (fact v 20 8).
{**morituros se potius quam ut rogaretur** (threat v 24 9).
{**irritaturum se potius quam ut efficiat** (likelihood vi 28 8).

THE MOODS

123. IMPERATIVE MOOD, with commands and prohibitions. The imperative has no third person in Latin, as in French and English. *Let him go* is **eat**: so even in the perfect: **poenas ille luerit** *let him have paid his due* Cic. *pro Mil.* 38 104 (**immo vero poenas ille debitas luerit; si ita necesse est, non debitas**). **Quamobrem hic nobis sit exceptus** *de Or.* i 38 172.

The **'future'** imperative as it was once called is an old form used on solemn occasions, and sometimes with mock seriousness: as, **transnanto Tiberim, somno quibus est opus alto** Hor. *S.* ii 1 8.

I, i nunc are often ironical. **I demens, et saevus curre per Alpes, Ut pueris placeas** Juv. x 166: **i nunc et iuvenis specie laetare tui** *ib.* 310. But not so in **I decus, i nostrum, et melioribus utere fatis** Virg. *Aen.* vi 546.

Other forms of **command. Non fugis hinc praeceps?** *Aen.* iv 565: **quin conscendimus equos?** Liv. i 57 4: **quin pacem exercemus?** Virg. *Aen.* iv 99: **quin tu fortunam confers?** Liv. ix 18 11: (**quin sic attendite** Cic. *pro Mil.* 29 78: **quin beneficium experiamur ei reddere** Ter. *Phorm.* iii 3 5): **quin potius primi sumus?** Tac. *Ann.* i 28: other instances Ter. *And.* iv 2 11, *Phorm.* iii 3 9, and Plaut. *Pers.* 275, *Most.* 383: **cur non potamus? quis eliciet?** Hor. *Od.* ii 11 13: **quis curat?** ii 7 23: **quis restinguet?** ii 11 18: **nil desperandum** i 7 27: **etiam taces?** Ter. *Ad.* iv 2 11: **scelerate, etiam respicis?** Plaut. *Pers.* 275: **etiam vigilas?** *Most.* 383: **etiam tu hinc abis?** Ter. *Phorm.* iii 3 9. Also by the future ind. **sec. 116.**

124. Prohibition is expressed by the 'abstract' perfect conjunctive with **ne**, literally meaning *suppose you do not*: stronger for being mildly suggested, like **facies ut sciam** *you may let me know*: rarely by imperative, with **ne** and **nec**: **nec tu mensarum morsus horresce** Virg. *Aen.* iii 394. See further under **sec. 128, 129.**

125. THE CONJUNCTIVE is the Mood of Desire and Thought. The difference between these two senses is often a matter of voice and intonation, or of the person used: **Restitissem?** *should*

I have resisted? **Restitisses** *you should*: the former is called **deliberative**, the latter **jussive**. Command however is never expressed directly by the conjunctive mood, except in the third person which is practically imperative. Even **cura ut valeas** is merely *mind your health*, though called Indirect Command.

126. The Conjunctive of Pure Thought is Conditional, Potential and Permissive or Concessive:

(*a*) **Conditional**: **roges, tuum labore quid iuvem meo** Hor. *Epod.* 1 15. **Partem opere in tanto, sineret dolor, Icare, haberes** Virg. *Aen.* vi 31. **Absque te foret** *but for you.* **Dixerit aliquis. Quaesierit sane. Dixerit haec Epicurus; non pugnem** Cic. *Fin.* v 27 80.

(*b*) **Potential. Ne** (**nae**) **ego libenter experiar**: **haud sciam** an for **haud scio an**: **quis Troiae nesciat urbem? quis crederet? quis dubitet? recenseam duces** Liv. ix 17 7: **quot duces nominem** 18 12. The apodosis of an abstract condition is potential. **Ut tu sis...non ego sim** *Suppose you were it would not follow that I should be* Hor. *Sat.* i 4 69.

The perfect Conjunctive like the Homeric optative *suggests* an **abstract** case, usually without time: as, **crediderim**: **fuerit melius**: **haud facile quis dispexerit** Tac. *Ann.* iii 22: **citius caruerimus** Liv. iii 52 8: **Ciceroni nemo ducentos nunc dederit nummos** Juv. vii 140: **Quis Martem...dignè scripserit?** Hor. *Od.* i 6 14: **Pace tuâ dixerim. Sed neque tum fuisse dubitaverim. Quorum neutrum adseveraverim** Tac. **Tu videris** *that will be for you to see*)(**ego videro** fut. perf. *you will find me attentive.*

127. Permissive or concessive. Luctere: multâ proruet cum laude Hor. *Od.* i 18 1: **emerserit; tenebitur** Cic. *ii Verr.* i 5 12: **fuerit ille L. Brutus: fuerit haec partium causa communis** *I care not if he were*, *Phil.* ii 30 75 (above **123**). **Milia frumenti tua triverit area centum: Non tuus hoc capiet venter plus ac meus** Hor. *S.* i 1 46. These differ from conditional uses in containing an element of time.

With the pluperfect. Fuisset, quem metui? Virg. *Aen.* iv

603: **decies centena dedisses: quinque diebus nil erat in loculis** Hor. *Sat.* i 3 15.

128. The Conjunctive of Will or Desire, so far as it is separate, may be called **Optative, Hortative** or **Deliberative.**

(*a*) **Prayer** is naturally imperative. **Da moenia fessis: da genus et mansuram urbem** says Aeneas Virg. *Aen.* iii 86: but addressing a stranger or a friend it is modestly expressed as a wish: **sis felix, nostrumque leves, quaecumque, laborem** i 330: **sis bonus o felixque tuis** *Ec.* 5 65. Time is rarely signified: as, **Hac Troiana tenus fuerit fortuna secuta** *Aen.* vi 62: **haec dicta sint patribus** Liv. vii 13 9: **nemo quemquam deceperit** ix 11 4: usually the perfect expresses an abstract **wish**: **quod di omen averterint** not in this case but generally. From a mild request it passes to an absolute **prohibition** in **Ne feceris** *suppose you do not* hence *do not* (rarely as, **nec quisquam ante significaverit** Tac. *Ann.* vi 34) (**sec. 124**).

129. (*b*) **Will** appears in the **second person** of the pres. tense only as general advice. **Ne tamen illi Tu comes exterior, si postulet, ire recuses: ultro non etiam sileas** Hor. *Sat.* ii 5 17, 90 (**non** for **ne** emphasises the word **sileas**). **Quid faciam praescribe. Quiescas** ii 1 5. **Saepe stilum vertas** i 10 73. In the third person usually with **ne**: but **nemo putet** Liv. v 44 1: **moratus sit nemo** ix 11 13. (**Ne forte recuses** means *lest perchance.*) In a **question** the idea is prominent rather than the will (**deliberative question**): **quid hoc homine facias?** Cic. *pro Sest.* xiii 29: **faveas tu hosti?** i.e. *the idea!* **Tu ad eum nihil referas?** *Phil.* ii 6 15 (**Te ut ulla res frangat** *Cat.* i 9 22 is essentially the same). **Quid ego oratione te flectam?** *Phil.* i 14 35. In indirect speech: **incitati sunt ut vobis praeirent quid iudicaretis** *to dictate your verdict*, *pro Mil.* 2 3.

(*c*) A **past duty** is expressed in the 'unreal' tenses either as a statement or as a question. **An ego non venirem contra alienum?** Cic. *Ph.* ii 2 3: **An mihi cantando victus non redderet?** Virg. *Ecl.* 3 21: **faces in castra tulissem** *Aen.* iv 604: **asservasses**

hominem Cic. *ii Verr.* v 65 168: **Quo graves Persae melius perirent** Hor. *Od.* i 2 22 (or potential '*would more rightly* fall'): **tibi uni peteres** Cic. *Phil.* ii 34 86: **at tu dictis Albane maneres** Virg. *Aen.* viii 643 vivid for *should have*: **frumentum ne emisses** Cic. *ii Verr.* iii 84 195. The following express either will or thought equally (*might* or *ought*): **fuisset** *Aen.* iv 603: **eadem me ad fata vocasses** *ib.* 678.

130. The **second person singular** in an indefinite sense (*you* = *anyone*) may take the Conjunctive in indicative sentences. Instances with **qui** and **si** Lucr. ii 41 42 314 849: **quoad licet ac possis** 850: **quae bene cognita si teneas, natura videtur** 1090. In Livy **antequam venias ad eum** ix 2 8: in Pliny *Ep.* **per noctem sonus ferri, et si attenderes acrius, strepitus..reddebatur** vii 27: though in this author the Conj. might have another source (**sec. 191**). Other instances **sec. 216.**

THE INFINITIVE

131. The prolative use (Infinitive with '*to*').

The Infinitive mood was perhaps the dative of a verbal noun, so that **donat habere, dederatque comam diffundere ventis** correspond to **dono dat, ludibrio habet.** The following verbs take the infinitive directly (**prolative infinitive**), omitting the commonest and the rarest: **audeo, vereor, non dubito, adsuesco** and **consuesco, constituo, instituo** and **statuo, decerno, cogito, paro, incipio, intermitto, omitto, supersedeo** (Madv.). Tacitus has: **M. Piso me repetere Syriam dehortatus est** *Ann.* iii 16: **perstitit incedere** as well as **pergo**: Cicero has **agere deterrebar** *i Verr.* 9 24 on the analogy of **prohibeo, veto** etc.: **habui dicere** *N. D.* iii 39 93 as well as **habui quae dicerem** *de Am.* iii 27. In poetry **maturo aggredior occupo erubesco** take inf. among many others. Horace uses it to express purpose and other relations: **Cuius octavum trepidavit aetas Claudere lustrum** *Od.* ii 4 24: **Marisque Baiis obstrepentis urges Summovere litora** ii 18 21: **Non hydra secto corpore firmior Vinci dolentem crevit in Herculem** iv 4

62: **pecus egit altos Visere montes** i 2 8. Virgil uses it often: **donat habere** above: **da sternere ferro corpus** *Aen.* xii 97 as direct object.

Iubeo and **volo** are transitive, but the infinitive is of the same nature as the above. **Impero** and **mando** are rare with inf.; **pecuniam solvi imperavi** Cic. *Att.* ii 4 1: **iubeo ut** is seldom used.

132. Instances with the **adjective** are **Non lenis recludere** Hor. *Od.* i 24 17: **impiger hostium vexare turmas** iv 14 22: **spernere fortior** iii 3 50: **quidlibet impotens sperare** i 37 10: **ferre iugum pariter dolosi** i 35 28: **furit te reperire atrox Tydides** *Od.* i 15 27. Tacitus has **dissentire manifestus** (sec. 9 above): Virgil **Quo non praestantior alter Aere ciere viros** *Aen.* vi 164: **boni...Tu calamos inflare** *Ec.* 5 2: **Certa mori** *Aen.* iv 564 (above l. 554 **certus eundi**): **maiorque videri** vi 49. With **nouns**, especially after **est**: **consilium est, tempus est, habere in animo, (in) animum induco**, in prose: **consilium cepi legari** Cic. *Att.* xiv 3 4, in poetry **amor, facultas, potestas, cupido est.** Without **est**: **proelia tentant...foedare** Virg. *Aen.* iii 241: **studium tueri** *Geo.* ii 195: **aetas pati** iii 60: **modus inserere** ii 73.

A copulative verb is followed by the infinitive with the same case as its own subject: as, **Malo fraterculus esse gigantis** Juv. iv 98. A passive verb governs a passive infinitive: as, **Urbs coepta est obsideri** (so **potest obsideri**, but **coepit fieri**). **Est vocari desitus** Cic. *Fam.* ix 21: **in lautumias deduci imperantur** *ii Verr.* v 27 68 (sec. 99).

The infinitive with passive verbs of saying and thinking has the same construction but rather belongs to the substantival infinitive: as, **secuturae sperabantur** Tac. *H.* ii 74: **Drusus defertur moliri res novas** *Ann.* ii 27.

133. The **Perfect Infinitive** is often used without time to express an act in its nature and effect on the mind, especially in wishes. **Iuvat fecisse: hoc te monitum volo: cui nihil negatum vellent: quem ego hominem honoris potius quam contumeliae causâ nominatum volo** Cic. *i Verr.* 7 18: **si pectore possit Excussisse deum**

Virg. *Aen.* vi 79: **tendentes Pelion imposuisse Olympo** Hor. *Od.* iii 4 52: **sapientia prima (est) Stultitiâ caruisse** *Ep.* i 1 42: **quiesse erat melius** Liv. iii 48 3: **mansum oportuit** Ter. *Haut.* i 2 26: **paeniteat trivisse** Virg. *Ec.* 2 34.

134. The Substantival Infinitive is the subject of impersonal verbs and phrases. **Iuvat ire et Dorica castra Desertosque videre locos** Virg. *Aen.* ii 27: **praeverti ad Armenios cura fuit** Tac. *Ann.* ii 55: **minari denique divisoribus ratio non erat** Cic. *i Verr.* 9 24: **inpudens postulatio visa est censere** Liv. xxi 20 4: **cuiusvis hominis est errare** (gen. of mark). **Religio est** and some above show that the origin of this use is the same as that of the direct infinitive.

The **predication** of which the infinitive is the subject may be direct as **Errare turpe est** or indirect as **errare turpe ducimus. Qui posse bellum geri pro victoria certâ haberent** Liv. ix 12 4. Very rarely the predication becomes an **attribution**: besides **tuum est scire** there is **scire tuum nihil est** *your knowledge is nothing* Pers. i 27: **Hoc ridere meum** i 122, even as the object of **vendo: ipsum dicere** Cic. *de Or.* i 24 112. When quoted as a word the inf. may have other constructions: **Inter optime valere et gravissime aegrotare nihil interesse** *Fin.* ii 13 43. [**Demeres necessitatem...te persequi** (Sall. *Jug.* 102) reminds one more of the inf. with **tempus est** etc. **132**.]

135. Historic Infinitive. This is a substantival infinitive with nominative subject but without incumbrance of person, number or time: **pars ducere muros, Molirique arcem et manibus subvolvere saxa** Virg. *Aen.* i 423. French *Ainsi dit le renard, et flatteurs d'applaudir* (see **sec. 108** for the two meanings).

It is usually detached from the sentence, but is sometimes found after 'inverse' or co-ordinate **quum** and other conjunctions: **Quum Tiberium anceps cura distrahere** Tac. *Ann.* ii 40: **non arma, non ordo, sed pecorum modo trahi** iv 25: **atque ipse adire municipia** ii 39. In Livy: **quum Appius...ius dicere** ii 27 1.

Rarely of past habit: **primus carpere** Virg. *Geo.* iv 134: **Te colere** *Aen.* iv 422.

THE GERUND AND GERUNDIVE

136. The Gerund usually expresses an action of the main subject, as **vires acquirit eundo** Virg. *Aen.* iv 175: but sometimes it is impersonal, as **nomen ipsum carendi** Cic. *Tusc.* i 36 87. Sometimes the object of the gerund is the same as the subject of the verb, so that the gerund appears to be passive: as **alitur vitium vivitque tegendo** Virg. *Geo.* iii 454: **lentescit habendo** ii 250: **cantando rumpitur anguis** *Ec.* 8 72: **ante domandum ingentes tollunt animos** *Geo.* iii 206. Or the gerund and verb have the same object and not the same subject: **pueros exercendi causâ producere** Liv. v 27 2.

137. The Gerundive takes the place of the transitive gerund: unless the object is a neuter adjective or pronoun for clearness as in **suum cuique tribuendo** Cic. *Br.* 21 85: **nihil nec vitando facere caute nec petendo vehementer** *Or.* 68 228: **inferiora populando** Tac. *Ann.* xv 38; or when there is some reason to separate the act from its object, or for convenience: as, **nec inferendo iniuriam nec patiendo** Liv. iii 53 9. **Equites tegendo** Liv. xxi 54 1 is the only instance of a transitive dative gerund: in the accusative it is also rare. **Purgandi sui causâ ad eum legatos mittunt** Caes. *b. g.* vi 9 6 may be accounted for by the following.

Noun and gerund in Apposition. This old construction may be the origin of the gerundive. **Facultas agrorum condonandi** Cic. *Phil.* v 3 6: **novarum spectandi copia** Ter. *Haut.* prol. 29.

Senescendorum hominum and **ad homines nascendos** are found in Varro, and may be compared with **volvenda dies** Virg. *Aen.* ix 7: and with **oriundus, contionabundus** etc. in support of an old *active gerundive.* But there are causal forms in **-sco**: **requierunt flumina cursus** Virg. *Ec.* 8 4: **insuevit me ut fugerem** Hor. *Sat.* i 4 105:

brachia consuescunt Lucr. vi 397. Compare **suetus, cretus, vietus** (Lucr.). Perhaps both forms are older than voice: comp. **143**.

138. Gerund of fitness and necessity. Here also may be observed an old transitive impersonal construction: **pacem Troiano a rege petendum** Virg. *Aen.* xi 230: **hac nocte mihi agitandumst vigilias** Plaut. *Trin.* 869: **aeternas quoniam poenas in morte timendumst** Lucr. i 111: **multa ciendum** iii 392: **addendumst partes alias** ii 492.

139. Accusative Gerund and Gerundive. Rarely used with **in, ante. Ante domandum** above: **ante conditam condendamve urbem** Liv. *praef.* 5. Compare **partis** and **petendis** below. With noun understood: **ad sepeliendos qui ciciderant** Liv. iii 43 6. **Faciendum loco, curo** belong to the ordinary gerundive rather than that of fitness and necessity: the object of care is not the necessary bridge but the construction, as appears more plainly in **cura pontis faciendi.**

140. Genitive of Gerund and Gerundive. Ars scribendi would be attributive gen.: *the art writing* or *the writing art*: **dicendi finem facere** (objective) Cic. *Sest.* 65 136. Very often to define the purpose of a noun: **paucis verbis carminis concipiendique iurisiurandi mutatis** Liv. i 32: **comitia auguris subficiendi** xxxix 45: **commorandi deversorium** Cic. *de sen.* 23 84, and the genitives with **locus** and **tempus** are of external definition (possessive) or attributive. Livy has **finiendae censurae actio** ix 33 5; and **vilia capita luendae sponsionis** ix 9 19 MSS. **sponsioni** Madvig: **oratores pacis petendae** ix 45 18: **deliberandi sibi** (compare **auctor** with the same genitive Liv. v 2 14) **unum diem postulavit** Cic. *N. D.* i 22 60. In the predicate **altera pars philosophiae quae est quaerendi** Cic. *Fin.* i 7 22: **quod unum exaequandae sit libertatis** Liv. iii 39: **concordiam ordinum quam dissolvendae tribuniciae potestatis rentur esse** v 3 5.

In Tacitus this genitive is used with verbs of an alleged or disputed motive: **ostentandae ut ferebat virtutis** *Ann.* iii 41 4: **vitandae suspicionis an quia** iii 9 2: **proficiscitur cognoscendae antiquitatis** ii 59 1. By extension he uses this genitive as a verb-noun in the nominative: **Vologeso penitus infixum fuit Romana arma vitandi** *Ann.* xv 5. Compare Greek Test. ὡς δὲ ἐγένετο τοῦ εἰσελθεῖν τὸν Πέτρον; but there can be no imitation.

Tacitus also uses the genitive gerund of advising and accusing. **Plancinam monuit Agrippinam insectandi** *Ann.* ii 43: **occupandae reipublicae argui** of a design to usurp vi 10. (He also has **accusans sinere.**)

141. Dative of Gerund and Gerundive. The dative Gerundive like the Genitive expresses the purpose of a Noun (dative sec. 32): **fatalis dux servandae patriae** Liv. v 19 2: **vinculum continendis sociis** xxi 52 8: **primum exstruendo tumulo caespitem** Tac. *Ann.* i 62 2: also of a noun and verb (sec. 31): **naves quas tutandis commeatibus habuerat** Liv. xxvii 15 5: **sanciendo, ut dictitabat, foederi convivium adicit** Tac. *Ann.* ii 65 4. The dat. gerund and gerundive may both be used with words of fitness: **facilis impetrandae veniae** Liv. xxvi 15 1: **verba excusandae valetudini solita** vi 22 7: **solita curando corpori** Tac. *Ann.* iii 15. With esse the gerund is rare: **oneri ferendo esse** Ov. *M.* xv 403: **solvendo non esse** only in Cic., as *Att.* xiii 10 1, *Phil.* ii 2 4.

142. Ablative of Gerund and Gerundive. This is properly abl. of the Instrument: but sometimes only of circumstance and almost temporal: **legationibus audiendis moratus** Liv. xxi 47 7: **miscendo consilia precesque orabant** ii 9 1: **partis honoribus eosdem gessi labores quos petendis** Cic. *Ph.* vi 6 17 (comp. **conditam** and **condendam** above): **athletas videmus nihil nec vitando facere cautè nec petendo** *Or.* 68 228: **pugnando vulnera passi** Virg. *Aen.* vi 660. **Invidit operi deterrendo** Tac. *Ann.* xiii 53. **Ultrà quam licet sperare nefas putando Disparem vites** Hor. *Od.* iv 11 30. **Primosque et extremos metendo stravit humum** iv 14 31. **Culpam gravi nomine maiestatis appellando suas leges egrediebatur** Tac.

Ann. iii 24. **Clamitando...munus suscepit** iii 31. **Accusandis senesceret** Liv. v 43 7 : **fando** Virg. *Aen.* ii 6 : **ordiendo** Tac. *Ann.* vi 8 : **obiectando** 38. The above use of the gerund explains the unchangeable so-called present participle in French which is really a gerund : *j'ai vu des femmes traînant leurs enfants* a-dragging. Expressing a standard : **cantando victus** Virg. *Ec.* 3 21 : abl. of respect : **violentior impediendo** Liv. vi 31 4 : with **ab** : **ordiar ab ducibus comparandis** ix 17 5.

The preposition **pro** occurs rarely with gerund or gerundive : **pro ope ferendâ sociis pergit ire** Liv. xxiii 28 11. **Sine** with **canendo** in Varro. With the comparative : **nullum officium rependendâ gratiâ magis necessarium est** Cic. *de Off.* i 15 47 ; with **contentus** : **possidendis agris contentos** Liv. vi 14 11 : and similarly **senatu regendo se tenuit** *was contented* xxiv 18 : **absistere sequendo** xxix 33. **In** is rare.

THE SUPINES

143. The Supine in -um is an Internal Accusative usually of Motion like **exsequias ire.** It may govern a case like a finite verb, as do other nouns. Motion is not always implied, as in **dare nuptum,** Ter. *And.* ii 1 1 : **sessum recipere,** Cic. *de Sen.* 18 63 : **herctum ciere** *summon to divide*, *de Or.* i 56 237.

The Supine in -u might sometimes be a dative, *e.g.* **turpe dictu** seems like **fortis spernere.** Again Plautus has **lepidum memoratui** *Bac.* 62. But **dictu** is not dative in **pudet dictu** Tac. *Agr.* 32, **dictu opus est** etc. The abl would be one of Respect, as in **grandis natu.** As to Voice, an abl. of respect would naturally be passive, but is not so in **gravis ictu,** Virg. *Aen.* v 274, **celeres proventu,** Plin. xiv 42 (Roby), **levis cursu** *Aen.* xii 489 : it is at all events intransitive.

THE PARTICIPLES

144. Participles in the plural masc. or neuter may be *used as Class-nouns*, as **ratione utentia** *reasonable beings* Cic. *de Off.* ii 3 11. So in the singular also, usually in oblique cases: especially in the genitive; sometimes with a noun understood, but often with an abstract meaning: **specie timentis**: **illecebrae peccantium**: **venerantium officia** *duties of homage*: **signa perculsi** *marks of panic*: **ambitio salutantium** *the pushing habit of making calls*: **altitudo nullis inquirentium spatiis penetrabilis** (*by no depth of sounding*) Tac. *Ann.* ii 61: **servientium patientiae taedebat** iii 65. Cicero would use a concrete noun: **sunt haec et alia falsi accusatoris signa** (*of collusion*). For participles as adjectives see below **147.**

145. The Present Participle. The participle of **sum** is supplied by words like **homo, mulier, adolescens. Facere enim probus adolescens periculosè quam turpiter pati maluit** Cic. *pro Mil.* 4 9: **sed homo sapiens atque altâ et divinâ quadam mente praeditus multa vidit** 8 21: **quum mulier fleret uberius, homo misericors** (*his feeling heart*) **ferre non potuit** *Ph.* ii 31. The Latin present participle is best translated by *while*, the English present participle often by **dum.**

146. The present participle sometimes relates to a **time just past or coming**, as **discedens dederam promissa** Virg. *Aen.* xi 46; **adveniens** *on arrival* Liv. xli 10 13:

To the end of a continuous act or state: **hanc multos florentem annos rex deinde...tenuit Mezentius** Virg. *Aen.* viii. 481: **eum primo implicantes responsis edocuerunt** Liv. xxvii 43 3: **multa movens animo Nymphas venerabar** Virg. *Aen.* iii 34: **per noctem plurima volvens...exire...Constituit** i 305: **omnia secum Versanti subito vix haec sententia sedit** xi 551: **urbem redeuntibus annis Condet** viii 47: **volventibus annis Romanos fore** i 234: **diem de die prospectans...iussit** Liv. v 48 3 (**cur oderit...patiens** Hor. *Od.* i 8 3 adj.).

To an act implied in another (*thereby* or *while*). **Conservans rationem nostram tueor** Cic. *Att.* i 17 10: **optimo animo utens nocet** ii 1 8: **offendere eius animum manens nolo** (*by remaining*) ix 13 4: **fratrem exheredans sec. 109.**

To a state interrupted or a purpose hindered: **arma ducum dirimens...maculavit sanguine Carrhas** Lucan i 104: **nec plura querentem passa Venus** *Aen.* i 385: **finienti restitit** Cic. *Att.* viii 3 3.

To a series of acts: **nusquam se aequo certamine committentes...tutabantur** Liv. iii 42 4: **verba vultus in crimen detorquens recondebat** Tac. *Ann.* i 7: **iterum remeante nuntio consulebatur** Liv. ix 3 7.

To a characteristic or typical act: **Demissa ab laevâ pantherae terga retorquens** Virg. *Aen.* viii 460: **tegumen torquens immane leonis** vii 666: **Aurea subnectens exsertae cingula mammae** i 492: **nubila dividens plerumque** (not now) Hor. *Od.* i 34 5.

147. Hence passing in to an attributive adjective of quality, though it may keep its verbal construction. **Voluptas elata et gestiens** Cic. *Tusc.* iii 10 23: **saxea effigies et vocalem sonum reddens** Tac. *Ann.* ii 61: **animans asper, acerba sonans, cui nomen asilo** Virg. *Geo.* iii 148: **arctos metuentes aequore tingi** i 246: **pascentem cycnos** ii 199: **iuga detrectans** iii 57: so **agens, eminens, ferens, valens, pallens, horrens, ardens** and many others. Virgil has **servantissimus aequi** *Aen.* ii 427 in adjectival construction: Lucr. **magis vitai claustra coercens** iii 397. A considerable number of course become complete adjectives, like **prudens** and **diligens.** (Tacitus uses the noun in **-tor**: **ceteris proemiorum ostentator** *Ann.* i 24: French *agent provocateur.*) As substantive **amans** etc.

148. The objective genitive usually takes the place of the accusative in the last instance but one: as in **metuens futuri** Hor. *S.* ii 2 110 like **capax imperii.** So **patiens, impatiens, impotens; retinens avitae nobilitatis** Tac. *Ann.* ii 30: **alieni adpetens, sui profusus** Sall. *Cat.* 5: **cupiens erogandae pecuniae** Tac. *Ann.* i 75. **The nom.**

form is often used with a picturesque effect in denoting **prominent** effort or attitude: (*a*) **venit hasta manu Stridens** Virg. *Aen.* ix 419: **clamor accidens** Liv. viii 39 4: **illa cadens** Virg. *Geo.* i 109: **adsurgens** *Aen.* i 535: **attollens** iv 690: **Ipse sinu prae se portans** xi 544. (*b*)**intuens**: **subridens** i 254: **reprehensans** and **obtestans** Liv. ii 10 3.

149. The Future Participle denotes

1. **Expectation.** **Tusculum se (miles)...fide misericordiâque victurus hospitum contulerat** Liv. iii 42 5. Passively: **melior futurus miles** xxi 21 11.

2. **Intention.** **In itinere adgregantur...animum ex eventu sumpturi** Tac. *Hist.* i 27. **Mare inferum petit oppugnaturus Neapolim** Liv. xxiii 1 5: **situ urbium se defensuri** viii 29 12: **fertur moriturus** Virg. *Aen.* vii 511. Passively: **caeso sparsuros sanguine flammam** (*intended to*) xi 82.

3. **Character.** **O nunquam dolituri** *Aen.* xi 732. **Da genus et mansuram urbem** iii 85. **Non missura cutem nisi plena cruoris hirudo** Hor. *A. P.* 476.

4. **The apodosis of a condition** (participle of the Conjunctive mood). **Daturus amplius si potuisset** Plin. *Ep.* iii 21. **Ad summa evasurus iuvenis nisi modicis contentus esset** (Roby from Seneca).

5. **Coordinate statement** in future time. **Quid metui moritura** *Aen.* iv 604. **Ceratis nititur pennis vitreo daturus nomina ponto** Hor. *Od.* iv 2 3.

6. Forming with its noun an **abstract substantive**: **nec te ...moritura tenet crudeli funere Dido** *the prospect of D.'s death*, *Aen.* iv 308.

150. For the **Perfect Participle** see under **Ablative Absolute.** It is often used **without time**: **solata** Virg. *Geo.* i 206: **molitus** 506: **amplexae** ii 367: **tonsis** iv 287: **circumdata** 497: **messae** *Aen.* iv 513: **mirata** vii 382: **abactae** viii 407: **raptas** 635: **epulata** iv 407: **solatus** v 708: **actis** viii 636.

ADVERBS TO INTERJECTIONS

ADVERBS

151. A few **qualifying adverbs** are: **sane** grudging or ironical: **ultro** *beyond expectation*: **dumtaxat** *just so*, coming to mean *at least* or *only*: **utique** *at least*, *in any case*, from **quisque**: **non utique** *not necessarily* Liv. viii 10 11: **porro** *aye, and more*: **non ita multo** (post), **non ita pridem** *not so very*: **tantum quod** *only just*, of time or degree: **tantum non** *all but.*

Adverbs of comparison: **perinde** *equally*, **non perinde** *not to the degree expected*: **proinde** *proportionately*, with imperative *accordingly.*

Of Time: **nunc....nunc, modo...modo** *at different times*: **modo** *lately* (**tam modo, inquit Praenestinus**): **aliquando** often means *at last*, **tandem** *I pray*: **prius** often apart from **quam**, with negatives always so: **cumque** Hor. *Od.* i 32 15 *on all occasions*: **subinde** *forthwith* or *from time to time*: **tantisper, paullisper** *just so long*, *for a short time*: **commodum** *just now*: **iam** of a higher degree; **iam verò** Cic. *de Imp.* 11 29: simple emphasis **iam istinc** Virg. *Aen.* vi 389: **iam inde** 385: climax **iam iam** iv 371 and Sall. *Jug.* 14 22.

Tum is used frequently in successive description: **tum silvis scaena coruscis** Virg. *Aen.* i 164: **tum violaria** etc. Hor. *Od.* ii 15 5.

152. **Of emphasis**: **denique** *in fact*, **tandem** *I pray*: **demum** (sometimes **denique**) for exclusive emphasis; **tum demum** *not till then*; **ea demum sponsio fuit** *that alone* Liv. ix 9 13: **tum denique vivemus** *then and not till then we shall live* Cic. *Tusc.* i 31 75. **En unquam?** adverb of **et quisquam?** **Vero** recalls or contrasts with emphasis after **tum, ille** etc.: **iam vero** (above) marks a climax: **tum vero** a critical moment: **at vero** a serious objection. **Ne** (**nae**) in **ne ille, ne tu** *believe me*: **ne illi vehementer errant** Cic. *Cat.* ii 3 6: **ne tu, si ita fecisses, melius famae consuluisses** *Ph.* ii 2 3 **Quidem** either with **qui** 'limiting' or with **et** merely adding an observation: **ille, tu quidem** in parenthesis followed by a disjunctive, as, **quaestio non satis prudenter illa quidem constituta, quaesitum est tamen** Cic. *Ph.* ii 9 22. **Adfatim** *enough*, **admodum** *very*, **oppido** *absolutely*,

omnino with an admission like Greek μέν. **Adeo** emphasises : **tres adeo sine sidere noctes** *Aen.* iii 203: expressing cause: **adeo, quanto rerum minus, tanto minus cupiditatis erat** Liv. *praef.* 8 : **atque adeo** *and what is more*: **ducem hostium intra moenia atque adeo in senatu videmus** Cic. *Cat.* i 2 5 : **adeo non** *much less*: **adeo ut** *to such an extent that*: **perquam** *extremely*: **p. breviter perstrinxi** *de Or.* iii 49 201.

153. Negatives. **Non** immediately precedes the word or phrase which it contradicts : **si non** granted a particular negative : followed by **non...saltem** = **ne—quidem.** **Haud** qualifies an extreme or uncomplimentary word : **haud ineptè, insulsè, absurdè** : or suggests a stronger expression by *litotes* and becomes a disguised superlative: **haud mediocris** for **singularis** Cic. *Rep.* ii 31 : **haud dubiè** *beyond all doubt*, **haud obscurè** *obviously*, **haud scio an** *I am inclined to think*: but **haud scio an aliquid simile visuris** in Plin. *Ep.* vii 19 *perhaps never* sec. 180. **Other negatives**: **aut nemo aut pauci** *few or none*; **aut nulli aut perpauci dies ad agendum futuri sunt** Cic. *i Verr.* 10 31 : **si minus** *if not*: **omnes tuos, si minus, quam plurimos**: **nunquam omnes hodie moriemur inulti** *assuredly not* Virg. *Aen.* ii 670 : **nusquam aliò** *to no other place* Liv. vii 8 7.

154. For **ne...quidem nec** is used in Juv. and Tacitus. **Ne... quidem** means *not even* or *not either*: like **nec** it strengthens a preceding negative: **nolite ne tirones quidem contemnere** Cic. *Phil.* xii 6 14. **Non modo** and **ne...quidem.** **Non modo cum clade ullâ sed ne cum periculo quidem suo** Liv. ix 19 14. It is usual to say that a **non** is omitted : but **non modo** rather means *not to say*, *to say nothing of*, as may be seen by the inverted form in **Ne sui quidem id velint, non modo ipse** Cic. *Tusc.* i 38 92. Liv. ix 6 8 **neque...non modo...elicere sed ne...quidem efficere poterant** is clear this way. The clause with **non modo** may be too weak or too strong : in the former case **sed etiam** follows, in the latter **ne...quidem.** **Non modo non** is used with **ne...quidem** where the predicate is different in the two clauses : but in Liv. xxv 26 10 **ut non modo lacrimis prosequerentur mortuos sed ne efferrent quidem.** In **non modo voce nemo sed ne vultu quidem assensus est** Cic. *Ph.* i 6 15 and in **neque** above, **ne...quidem** strengthens the negative preceding. In questions the following is regular: **quo tempore aut quâ in re non modo ceteris specimen dedisti sed tute tui periculum fecisti?** Cic. *div. in Caec.* 8 27: the question being equivalent to another negative.

The same idea is expressed by **nedum** *much less*, **ne** with conjunctive Liv. iii 52 9, **tantum abest ut...ut...**, and **atque adeo** above.

155. Interrogative particles. **An** properly introduces a second question, often unreal or exaggerated: hence it is used with all exaggerated questions. Plautus uses **an** with a single indirect question: so also Tac. and Juvenal. **Respicit an tibi servi octo** (late use without verb) Juv. vii 141: **nescio an** under **indirect question** 180. **An** is sometimes equivalent to **sive**: **litteris ex Epiro an Athenis datis** Cic. *Att.* vii 1 9 (reading dub.), **Octavius est an Cornelius quidam** *Fam.* vii 9 3 and frequently in Tacitus. On the other hand **dubii seu vivere credant Sive extrema pati** Virg. *Aen.* i 218 and elsewhere. Questions may be asked without particle: when the speaker's words are repeated (indirect question) or when the tone suffices: **Miremur? si** Liv. ix 18 10: **non dices?** Hor. *Sat.* ii 7 21: **ego eum non tuear?** Cic. *Planc.* 39 93: this is common in Tacitus.

Alternative questions. **Utrum** may be omitted when the issue is really simple. **Auditis an me ludit amabilis insania?** Hor. *Od.* iii 4 6: **Filius, anne aliquis?** Virg. *Aen.* vi 864: **linquontur necne?** Lucr. iii 713: **quid? vos duas habetis patrias? an...**Cic. *leg.* ii 2 5: **rara sit an densa requires** Virg. *Geo.* ii 227. So in the indirect question with **interest** etc.: **refert consul an dictator** Liv. ix 9 7: **doleam necne doleam nihil interesse** Cic. *Tusc.* ii 12 29: **in incerto erat vicissent victine essent** Liv. v 28 5. Both particles may be omitted where balance exists: **Nec discernatur interdiu nocte... pugnent** Liv. viii 34 10. **Aut** repeats the first question in a different usually a stronger form: **Creditis avectos hostes? aut ulla putatis Dona carere dolis Danaum?** *Aen.* ii 43.

Numne Cic. *de Am.* 11 36, comp. **utrumne** etc. **91**: **anne** for **an** *Pis.* 1 3.

Answers. To **ita, sane** etc. add **optimè** *with pleasure*: **benignè** *no thank you* (ἐπαινῶ): **immo** is often followed by **verò** (Greek μὲν οὖν).

CONJUNCTIONS

156. **Que...et** so common elsewhere is not used by Cicero except in *Fam.* xv 7. Instead he uses **quum...tum**, with the indicative except in a contrast or with a difference of time: also **quâ...quâ** (**Quâ cibi quâ quietis** Liv. ix 3 4). **Quum** may be followed by **tum praeterea** *and in particular*, **tum maximè** *and especially*: **dicimus C. Verrem quum multa nefariè fecisset tum praeterea quadringenties sestertium in Sicilia contra leges abstulisse** Cic. *i Verr.* 18 56. **Que** after a negative where **sed** might have been used: **Non tamen omnes...excedunt pestes, penitusque necesse est** Virg. *Aen.* vi 737: **tellus extendere litora nolet Excutietque fretum** Lucan i 77. Sometimes **que** has the sense of 'inverse' **quum**: **vix ea fatus erat subitoque fragore Intonuit laevum** Virg. *Aen.* ii 692. **Que** in Virg. is used to join unbalanced words: **gravis graviterque** *Aen.* v 447: **comitem et propinquum** ii 86: **obvius adversoque** x 734. **Et** sometimes means '*and that*' **Et recte.** It may express indignation: **Et quisquam numen Iunonis adorat Praeterea?** *Aen.* i 48. **Et dubitant?** *Geo.* ii 433. Or=*and yet* **avidum et minorem** Tac. *Ann.* i 13: **turbidos et nihil ausos** i 38; or *and indeed*: in *parataxis* instead of a temporal connection Virg. *Aen.* iii 5. **Atque** emphasizing apodosis: **si brachia remisit, Atque illum...rapit alveus** *Geo.* i 203.

157. **Nec...et** with meaning *but* *Ec.* 7 16. **Nec** *nor indeed*: **nec mirum**: **nec fefellit** Liv. ii 19 7. *But not*: **flet si lacrimas conspexit amici Nec dolet** Juv. iii 102. For **ne...quidem** *not even*, *not either*, in Tacitus and Juvenal, perhaps Horace, and Cicero. **Quâ deterius nec Ille sonat, quo mordetur gallina marito** Juv. iii 90: **nec nunc quum me vocat ultro Accedam?** Hor. *S.* ii 3 261 (v.l. **ne** less likely): **nec cellis ideo contende Falernis** Virg. *Geo.* ii 96: *not either* in **nullâ exspectatâ nec quaesitâ voluptate** Cic. *Fin.* ii 26 82. **His nec amor causa est** Virg. *Ec.* 3 102. **Nec** does not contradict a preceding negative: **nemo neque poeta neque orator fuit** Cic. *Att.* xiv 20.

158. **Aut...aut** exclude all other alternatives but those given: **proinde aut exeant aut quiescant** Cic. *Cat.* ii 5 11. **Aut** in questions under **an** above: **aut saltem** *or at least.* **Aut** *or else*: **neque...dare...neque...lavere...aut exanimari** Hor. *Od.* i 4 3. **Vel** *if you please* of things indifferent: **hunc ordinem vel paci decorum vel bello** Liv. i 42 3: **vel qui venit** Virg. *Ec.* 3 50 *if you will*: **omnia vel medium fiat mare** 8 59. **Vel quum** without apodosis in exclamation: **Vel quum se pavidum contra mea iurgia fingit** *Aen.* xi 406: **vel quae** *Ec.* 9 21. **Seu** *whether* is often omitted (sec. 51.)

159. **Sed** *but* usually after negative or **ille quidem, tu quidem** (above): or, *to resume*, especially with **tamen** = δ' οὖν. In late Latin **sed** of an emphatic afterthought: **scalis habito tribus sed altis** Martial i 116 7: **Boletus domino, sed quales Claudius edit** Juv. v 147: **sed Buten averso corpore** Virg. *Aen.* xi 690.

Verum always means *but* and always comes first: **verò** never begins a clause. **Ceterum** passes to a new topic. **Nam** often dismisses an obvious reflection (*you need not tell me*). **Nam quod scribis te audire** (*i.e.* that I am mad)...**mihi verò mens integra est** Cic. *Att.* 3 13. **Nam te nec sperent Tartara regem** Virg. *Geo.* i 36. **Autem** adds a circumstance or is a simple *but.* **Sed** with it in **sed quid ego haec autem nequidquam ingrata revolvo** *Aen.* ii 101. **Atqui** is a logical *but* introducing the last step but one in a proof. **Nunc** *but as it is* after an unreal condition. *But* in antithesis is expressed by the arrangement of words (**chiasmus**): **Video meliora proboque: deteriora sequor** Ov. *Met.* vii 21.

160. **At** or **at enim** (ἀλλὰ νὴ Δία) of an objection mentioned only to be refuted. **At enim solidum est ut me Siculi maximè velint: illud vero obscurum est**...(at including both clauses) Cic. *div. in Caec.* 7 22. **At venit cum subscriptoribus exercitatis et disertis** 15 47. **At enim Cn. Pompeius rogatione suâ et de causâ iudicavit** *I shall be told*, *pro Mil.* vi 15. **At valuit odium, fecit inimicus** xiii 35. This may be answered by the speaker's **at**, making a succession of counter-arguments. **At**

hercule in a confidential outburst: *to tell you candidly* or *between ourselves you know* (**hercle quî** Plaut. *Trin.* 464). **At etiam** frequent in *Phil. ii* of a new aggravation of the offence. **Etenim** *moreover, and again*: **enimvero** indignant emphasis: **enim** may emphasize only. **Quam pius Aeneas tibi enim, tibi, maxima Iuno, Mactat** Virg. *Aen.* viii 84: **Namque, fatebor enim** *Ec.* I 32. **Namque** is often second in Virgil and always in Tacitus.

PREPOSITIONS

161. The following uses are worth mention.

Accusative. **Ad.** **Ad duo milia et trecenti** Liv. x 17 8: **occisis ad milibus quattuor** Caes. *b.g.* ii 33 5: **ad assem** *to the last penny*: **ad summam** *in short.*

Of external relations and standards, opp. of **in**: **ad famam concurrunt**: **ad famam dilectus haberi coeptus** Liv. ix 7 7: **ad gloriam accendi**: **ad hunc modum** Cic. *Tusc.* ii 4 10: **ad naturam**: **ad speciem** *to the eye*: **ad unguem** *to perfection*: **ad diem ad tempus ad quartam** *to the hour* or '*by the clock*' (**in quartam** of an appointment): **interest ad**: **multo minus ad nos**: **nihil ad Atticum** *no relation to A.* or *no comparison.* In Tac. **ornatum ad urbis**: **ad manum** *at hand*: **ad terrorem** *in consequence of alarm.*

Apud: of place, correct but rare: **apud Regillum**: **apud villam**: **apud Issum**: **apud oppidum** Caes.: **apud aedem** old decree *de Bacan.* Usually with persons or companies: **apud me valet**: **apud prudentes extollebatur** Tac. *Ann.* i 9: **Misenum apud et Ravennam** iv 5.

162. **Ante**: *in front of* or *facing*: **ante muros** of the attack: opposite of **pro** defending: **ante diem tertium** *three days before*

Post: **sextum post cladis annum** Tac.: **post diem tertium quam** or **eius diei** Cic.: **postridie ludos**: **post hominum memoriam** *within living memory or human record.* Often local.

Circum in Cic. usually, **circa** in Livy: **circa viam, flumen** *by* *the road or river*: **omnia circa : publica circa bonas artes socordia** Tac. *Ann.* xi 15: **circa sex horas : circiter** adv. only.

Citra: *less than*; **citra scelus** Ov. : **citra spem** opp. to **praeter spem.**

Erga: only of feeling and always friendly: Fr. *envers* or *pour* not *vers.*

Extra: extra culpam *beyond reproach.*

Inter : of class: **pax inter temulentos** *a drunken peace*: **aleam inter seria exercent** *as a pursuit*: **damnari inter sicarios** *to be convicted of murder*: *at a time of*; **inter cenam : inter sanguinem et vulnera** Liv. ix 40 6: **inter decem annos** *in the course of ten years* Cic. *de imp.* 23 68. **Amisiam et Lupiam amnes inter** Tac. *Ann.* i 60 : **Faesulas inter Arretiumque** Liv. xxii 3 3: **inter paucas memoranda clades** xxii 7 1.

Infra and **supra** of different levels: **infra Lycurgum** *since Lycurgus* Cic. *Brut.* 10 40: later **supra hominem** *superhuman*: **paullo supra hanc memoriam** *a little before our day* Caes. *b.g.* vi 19 4.

Iuxta *next to*, *following upon*: **iuxta divinas res humanam fidem colere** Liv. ix 9 4: **consuetudo iuxta vicinitatem** *due to* xxxix 9 6.

Ob : *in payment for* (old Latin): **ob rem iudicandam pecuniam accipere** legal phrase Cic. *ii Verr.* ii 32 78. Not cause but motive: **ob eam rem scripsi : cuius ob auspicium infandum...videmus consedisse urbem luctu** *for the sake of* not *because of* Virg. *Aen.* xi 347 : **nec meliores ob scientiam facti** *none the better for* Cic. *Rep.* i 19: in local sense: **ob oculos versari** *pro Rab.* 14 39.

Penes : *at the door of*, Fr. *chez*: **penes te laus, culpa, arbitrium, victoria, noxa** Liv. ix 1 6: **causas adferebat, potissimum penes incuriam paucorum** Tac. *Ann.* iv 16.

163. Per: manner not cause: **per summum dedecus** *most shamefully*: **per vim** *with violence*: **per tumultum omnia aguntur** *the air is full of revolution*: **per timorem** *in fear*, §§ **49, 55.**

Of an obstacle: **per eum stetit quominus: per me licet** *I do not forbid*: **quod si per furiosum illum tribunum senatui quod**

sentiebat perficere licuisset; novam quaestionem nullam habuissemus Cic. *pro Mil.* vi 15: **petis ut per me liceat quendam de exsilio reducere** *Ph.* ii 4 9: **per aetatem ad pugnam inutiles** Liv. ii 16 4 (but not **utiles**): **qui per aetatem ire possent** *not prevented* Caes. *b. g.* vii 71 2: **per famam et populum nigros efferre maritos** Juv. i 72 *in spite of*: **per tela per hostes** Virg. *Aen.* ii 664: **petunt per vulnera mortem** *Geo.* iv 218.

Distributively: **per oppida custodiri: it Fama per urbes: invitati hospitaliter per domos** Liv. i 9 9.

In entreaty: **per ego has lacrimas dextramque tuam te...oro** Virg. *Aen.* iv 214.

Of time: **per idem tempus: per somnum.**

Praeter: *past, beyond*: **praeter spem, opinionem, solitum, modum, aequales:** in Cic. elliptically or as adverb: **praeter hominum perpaucorum** *Q. F.* i 1 5: **praeter damnatis** Sall. *Cat.* 36: **praeter amasse** Ov. *H.* vii 164: **praeter plorare** Hor. *Sat.* ii 5 69.

Prope: prope metum res fuerat: propius, proximè also govern the accusative as well as dative: **proxime hostem** Cic. *Att.* vi 5 *fin.*

Secundum: secundum naturam vivere: secundum deos violati sumus *next to* Liv.: **secundum praelium** *after the battle* Liv.: **secundum binos ludos** Cic. *i Verr.* 11 34.

Versus: more usually with **ad: ad Oceanum versus:** but **Romam versus.**

164. Ablative. **A, ab** (**ab nobis** *from us*, **a nobis** *by us*): of distance: **a quattuor milibus inde** Liv.: **ex eo loco a milibus passuum circiter duobus** Caes. *b. c.* v 32 1.

Agent, author or source: **a naturâ ita generati sumus** Cic. *Off.* i 29 103: **salvebis a meo Cicerone: timere ab aliquo: ab aestu relictae naves** Caes.: **pecuniam ab Egnatio** (banker) **solvere** Cic. *Att.* vii 18 4: **scribe decem a Nerio** Hor. *Sat.* ii 3 69: **inops a longâ obsidione** Liv. ii 14 3: **a saturis fabulam** vii 2 8: **ab radice ferens cupressum** Virg. *Geo.* i 20: **ab Româ,** see abl. case **sec. 40.**

Of time: succession unbroken: **ab horâ iii bibebatur: ab hâc**

contione legati missi sunt Liv. xxiv 22 3: **ab ovo usque ad mala** *from start to finish* Hor. *Sat.* i 3 6: **secundum a Romulo** Liv. vii 1 10.

Of direction: **a senatu, a Caesare stare: timere a suis: quattuor addunt quattuor a ventis fenestras** Virg. *Geo.* iv 298: **servus a manu** *a secretary*: **servus a pedibus** *a footman*: **mediocriter a doctrinâ instructus** Cic. *Brut.* 53 198. So **inde, unde.**

Clam: also as adverb: in comedy with accusative.

Palam: also adverbial.

Sine: sine omni fraude, so **sine iniuriâ utriusque** Liv. vii 21 8, less commonly **ullâ:** once only with gerundive, rarely with participle: **sine restitutâ potestate** Liv. iii 52 2, **sec. 142.**

165. **De: de** became at last the sign of the genitive as in French. It always implied the sense of belonging, as in compounds **debeo, demo, dedo.** It is used

with a person or thing concerned: **bene mereri de: quid de nobis fiet? de nobis facile est** *never mind about us.*

of a number, quantity or substance to which something belongs: **unus de multis** *one like many others*: **homo de plebe: de exercitu quinquaginta caesi: unus de praetoribus: de parvo, de meo emere, sumere: de marmore signum** *a marble image.*

of a proper place, time or standard: **de caelo tonare, de caelo spectare** *look for omens in the sky*: **de loco superiore agere: de viâ** *by the way*: **eripere de** (or dative): **extorquere de manibus, avellere de matris complexu, exire de vitâ (excedere e vitâ): partem solido de die** Hor. *Od.* i 5 20: **de meâ voluntate fecit** (like **ex sententiâ**): **de integro** etc.: **de die vivere** *to feast by daylight*: **de mense Decembri** *before December is over*: **diem de die exspectare, differre.**

166. **E, ex: ex** before almost all consonants and always before **me, te, se.**

Perhaps coincidence is the most general meaning: then origin, succession, and contrast.

E regione *in a line*: **e vestigio** *au pied du moment*: **ex animo, ex sententiâ, ex parte, ex asse** *wholly*, **ex tempore** *appropriately*: **ex**

improviso *suddenly*: **heres ex asse** *heir to the whole*: **e republicâ** *for the good of the commonwealth.*

Of **origin**: **aeger ex vulnere: ex insidiis interire, ex quo fit: ex Miseno, ex Siciliâ: spero ex te aliquid, poculum ex auro, quaero ex, accipio ex.**

Succession: **ex hoc die, ex consulatu profectus** Cic. *Brut.* 92 318: **motum ex Metello** Hor. *Od.* ii 1 1 not *ever since* but *then beginning*: **bella ex bellis serere: ex pace bellum: dii ex hominibus facti** *men became gods*: **hominum ex facie Induerat in voltus... ferarum** Virg. *Aen.* vii 19: **diem ex die exspectare** (like **de**).

Contrast: *one alone among many*, **unum ex multis** (but **unus multorum**): **delecti e civitate.**

167. Prae: causal after a negative: **solem prae iaculorum multitudine non videbis** *in the face of* Cic. *Tusc.* i 42 101 : or with negative implied: **prae indignitate silentium patres defixit** Liv. vi 40 1: **non hiscere quenquam prae metu** ix 16 12: **impotens prae seditionibus** ix 14 5.

Of **place** mostly metaphorically: **prae se ferre** *to profess*: less common literally: **stillantem prae se pugionem ferens** *displaying.*

Of **comparison with a superior,** often ironically: **Romae prae Capuâ irridere** Cic. *leg. agr.* ii 35 96: **prae nobis beatus es** *Fam.* iv 4.

Pro *on* and *facing away from*: **pro rostris** *from the tribune*: **pro ripâ** *with their backs to the river*: so **pro munimentis, pro turribus, pro tribunali, pro suggestu** *on the platform.*

In a **certain character,** with abl. of the person or office: **pro hoste habere: pro consule** *with consular powers*: **pro suffragio, imperio creare, agere: pro auctoritate meâ hortor: pro tribu fieri** *to receive vote of tribe*: **pro imperio** of real or assumed office Liv. ii 56 12: so **satis pro imperio, quisquis es** Ter. *Phormio* i 4 19: **pro testimonio mentiri** *to give false evidence* Cic. *in Vat.* 1 3.

In proportion: **pro se quisque: pro viribus: pauci** (or **pauciores quam**) **pro numero hostium. Proelium atrocius quam pro numero**

pugnantium Liv. xxi 29 2: **pro malis recte** (*considering*) Cic. *Att.* xii 15.

Cum *of mutual relations*: **Maecenas quomodo tecum?** Hor. *Sat.* i 9 42: especially with verbs like **pugno, certo** (dat. in poetry), **ago**; with **par** and **impar**, and to mark equality or contrast, as **Remo cum fratre Quirinus, hostes cum civibus**: of appendages: **cum telo esse, cum v cohortibus** (*in command of*); and circumstances (abl. of manner).

Tenus: tenus includes the part mentioned: **crurum tenus** *right up the leg*: **capulo tenus** *hilt and all*: **verbo tenus** *literally and no further.*

168. With both Cases.

In with accusative signifies intention or extension.

Direction intended: mittere in exsilium: irasci in cornua: in clipeum assurgat: in longitudinem: aries in cornua tortus Manilius ii 245: **carmen in aliquem scribere.**

Manner or effect intended: in has leges ictum foedus Liv. xxiii 34 1 (**ad** would imply existing **leges**): **iurare in verba** *swear to obey*, not swear to his oath: **consensum in omnem formam luctus** ix 7 8: **crescere in ventrem** Virg. *Geo.* iv 122: **in numerum** *keeping time*: **in conditionem venerunt** *came to agreement*: **in hunc modum** as well as **ad**: comp. Tac. **dissimilis in dominum** *Ann.* ii 39, others **sec. 24; excisum latus rupis in antrum** Virg. *Aen.* vi 42: **se nux induet in florem** *Geo.* i 188.

Time intended (duration or date): **edicere in sextum diem: in sex menses dictator dictus: in Kalendas comítia edicta: vocare ad cenam in posterum diem.**

With words not of time this is rare: **venire in funus** *to arrive for the funeral* Cic. *Att.* xv 16 1: **distulit in seram commissa piacula mortem** Virg. *Aen.* vi 569.

Extension or distribution: argenti pondo et selibras in militem Liv. xxii 23 6: **in dies maius** *increasing daily*: **in aestatem crescit** *advances with the summer*: **in plebem ventura omnia** vi 13 11: **addunt in spatia** *quicken with each round* Virg. *Geo.* i 513.

In old phrases **in** with the acc. is used for **place without motion**: **in ditionem** or **potestatem esse**: **in amicitiam esse**: quoted n Livy and Cicero: **in potestatem habere** Sall. *Jug.* 112 3.

169. **In** ablative: **identity** with a class: **in pretio est** *it is of value*: **in deliciis habere**: **examenque improbum in illâ castiges trutinâ** Pers. i 7: **in difficili esse, in ambiguo, in pueris**: **hoc erat in votis** Hor. *Sat.* ii 6 1: **in imagine** *under a semblance*: **multum in parvo**: **res in praeda captas** Liv. ix 1 5: **in culpâ est animus** Hor. *Ep.* i 19 13: **in indutiis res fuisset** Liv. ix 9 13.

Place: **in manibus** *within reach* (*in the hand* is **intra manus**): **spem ponere in.**

Dress: **in flore novo** Virg. *Geo.* iv 142: **tenerâ in herbâ** i 112.

Case or circumstance: **in tempore** *at the right time*: **talis in hoste fuit Priamo** Virg. *Aen.* ii 541: **dolus an virtus quis in hoste requirat?** *ib.* ii 390: **in summâ caritate annonae**: **in variis voluntatibus** (*in the midst of disagreement*) **regnari tamen omnes volebant** Liv. i 17 3. **Densa sere: in denso non segnior ubere Bacchus** *on the crowded system* Virg. *Geo.* ii 275: **in corpore adfecto vigebat vis animi** Liv. ix 3 5: **certamina ponit in ulmo** Virg. *Geo.* ii 520.

Time: **in sex diebus perficere aliquid** (or **intra**, or abl. only): but **in tempore, in praesentia** *under fit or present circumstances.*

170. **Sub**: of **time**: **sub adventum consulis**: in Caesar **sub ipsâ profectione** (*b. c.* i 27 3).

Of **place**: **sub moenia** *up to the walls*: **sub antro, sub Tartara** *down in, down into*: **sub ipso** of place *next* Virg. *Aen.* v 322.

In **composition** **sub** means *up*: **succendo** *light up*, **succresco** *crop up* Plaut. *Trin.* 31 etc., **succurro** *run up*, **subeo** *come up*, **submitto** *send up.*

Super in prose never means *upon* and rarely takes the abl. (**solio sedet, in mensâ stat**): with the accusative it expresses motion over: **super alta vectus Attis celeri rate maria** Catullus lxiii 1: *beyond* poetical for **supra**: **super et Garamantas et Indos** Virg. *Aen.* vi 794: **super morbum fames** Liv. xxviii 46 15: **super lx milia** Tac. *G.* 63:

super omnia Liv. xxxi 18 3: *above* without motion: **Nomentanus erat super ipsum** Hor. *Sat.* ii 8 23. The abl. is poetic or colloquial: **fronde super viridi** Virg. *Ec.* 1 80: **super his** *besides* Hor. *Sat.* ii 6 3: **hac super re scribam** Cic. *Att.* xvi 6 1.

171. To the prepositions[1] partly belong **susque deque: procul** abl. So **simul nobis habitat** Hor., Ov., Tac.: **tali intus templo** Virgil *Aen.* vii 192: **insuper his** abl. ix 274. **Usque** is an adverb: **usque Romam** but **usque ad urbem.**

The prepositions **ad, ob, ab, sub,** are never joined with **-que.**

172. INTERJECTIONS. Strictly speaking, interjections are not language at all, but more or less articulate expressions of emotion; voluntary or involuntary movements of the lungs and speech-organs arising from physical causes or from association.

The Cases used in connection with Interjections have really to do with the thought or emotion, and not with the interjection, which is a parenthesis. The Nominative denotes the subject of the emotion, the Accusative the direct object: the Vocative is used of the person addressed, the Dative of the person interested. The Genitive marks the cause or person to which the feeling relates: compare **heu facti, foederis heu taciti, pro deum immortalium** with **poenitet me facti, pudet me facinoris** or **patris.**

SUBORDINATE AND CO-ORDINATE CLAUSES

173. These are usually distributed into **Substantival, Adjectival** and **Adverbial.** It will be more convenient to take in their turn the forms of Indirect Speech with connected idioms, the whole of the relative clause, and the clause with conjunctions, including substantival **quod** and **ut.**

174. INDIRECT SPEECH mainly uses two forms of **Substantival Clause.**

The abstract substantival clause, consisting of a **noun with a participle,** or **its equivalent,** plays a great part in

[1] A preposition by definition should admit of being compounded with a verb.

Tacitus. **Agrippina spem male tegens** *the ill-concealed hopes of Agrippina*, *Ann.* iv 12 2: **filius legati orator** *the choice of their commander's son for an envoy* i 19: **nihil nisi atrox terrebat** xii 35: **extrema iam salus et adsistentes matres...addunt animos** iv 51: **angebant ingentis spiritus virum Sicilia Sardiniaque amissae** Liv. xxi 1 5: **diu non periclitatum tenuerat dictatorem** vii 8 5: **notumque furens quid femina possit** *the knowledge* etc. Virg. *Aen.* v 6: **moverat eum subeunda dimicatio** *the necessity of facing a struggle* Liv. ii 13 2: **occisus Caesar pessimum facinus videretur** Tac. *Ann.* i 8: **moritura tenet...Dido** *the prospect of Dido's fate* Virg. *Aen.* iv 308: **ecquid et pater Aeneas...excitat** iii 343. This occurs in various cases. **Spretae iniuria formae** *Aen.* i 27: **spes surgentis Iuli** x 524: **fragor rupti pontis** Liv. ii 10 10: **ira diremptae pacis** ix 8 12: **virorum vox tota erat tribuniciae potestatis ereptae** iii 48 9: **exitium magnum atque Alpes immittet apertas** Virg. *Aen.* x 13: **cui nunquam exhausti satis est** *Geo.* ii 398: **ante conditam condendamve urbem** Liv. *praef.* 5: **ante expectatum** Virg. *Geo.* iii 347: **queror amissos exercitus: captae superavimus urbi** *Aen.* ii 643: **opus est facto: turpis coniuge barbarâ** Hor. *Od.* iii 5 5: **te duce: nec opinato** and other ablatives of circumstance: **plenum Nerone propinquo** *his kinship with Nero* Juv. viii 72.

175. An ingenious form of indirect speech thus arises, where a number of these phrases are subjects of some verb such as **dicebantur. Nec domesticis abstinebatur: abducta uxor: consulti pontifices: luxus Pollionis: gravis in rempublicam mater, gravis noverca** Tac. *Ann.* i 10: and more in ch. 9 with the verb **celebrabantur** expressed. Sometimes there is no verb, as in i 41, **quis ille flebilis sonus? quod tam triste?...pudor inde et miseratio...Augusti avi memoria...socer Drusus, ipsa insigni fecunditate** etc.

176. The Indirect Statement by a **Substantive and Infinitive.** This is found in apposition, even with an ablative: **disputavisse de hoc ipso, nihil esse bonum** Cic. *Tusc.* ii 25 61. In the Passive the noun is nominative and the infinitive is reckoned prolative, but should belong here.

In poetry a Greek idiom is followed: **phaselus ille quem videtis, hospites, ait fuisse navium celerrimus** Cat. iv 1: **rettulit Aiax esse Iovis pronepos** Ov. *Met.* xiii 141: **gaudent perfusi sanguine fratrum** Virg. *Geo.* ii 510, might be explained as two statements, but is apparently the same as **gaudent in tristi funere fratris** Lucr. iii 72: so probably **sensit medios delapsus in hostes** Virg. *Aen.* ii 377, an imitation of ᾔσθετο, so **fallit sorte beatior** Hor. *Od.* iii 16 32, in imitation of λανθάνει ὤν. So **dissentire manifestus** Tac. *Ann.* xi 57. On the other hand **Uxor invicti Iovis esse nescis** Hor. *Od.* iii 27 73 may mean *you do not know how to play the part*, **sec. 9.**

Verbs of hoping take the accusative and future infinitive: but **spero me posse** of indefinite time: **spero esse ut volumus** Cic. *Att.* xii 6 *fin.* Tacitus omits **se: speravit adsecuturum:** so Liv. xxxi *praef.* 2 **profiteri ausum perscripturum. Memini** takes the pres. inf. of a continuous act., **praedicere, contendere** Virg. *Ec.* 7 79; end of **sec. 110.**

177. Mene incepto desistere victam Virg. *Aen.* i 37 is a **Substantival Clause without construction** expressing indignation; with the corresponding **ut**-clause **te ut ulla res frangat! sec. 204.** Compare the French *moi t'abandonner!*

178. Indirect Command in the infinitive with **iubeo** belongs to the **Prolate Infinitive.** The pres. conj. is used after pres. and future, and the imperfect in narrative, **sec. 119—122.** Conj. without particle: **Vetabo solvat** Hor. *Od.* iii 2 26, and with **quaeso, opto.**

179. Fearing. There is no indicative form as in Greek for apprehension as to fact past, present or future. **Vide ne illa causa fuerit appellandi mei** Cic. *Ph.* ii 12 28. Translate **metuo ut** *I fear as to his doing*, that is generally, *I fear he will not do.* (But when the **ut**-clause comes first, it is found in the opposite sense. **Ut ferulâ caedas...non metuo** Hor. *Sat.* i 3 120.) Compare **videte ut respondere posse videamur** Cic. *de imp.* 23 68, implying *I fear we cannot*: **videas ut honestum sit** *i.e. I fear it is not*, *Att.* vii 14 3.

180. INDIRECT QUESTION. Virgil certainly would seem to use **seu** in Indirect Questions. **Substitit erravitne viâ seu lassa resedit Incertum** *Aen.* ii 740: **spemque meumque inter dubii seu vivere credant,** etc. i 218. **Si** is also found in questions in Livy, **quaesivere si liceret** xl 49 6. Plautus has **ibo visam si domi est** Ter. *Haut.* i 1 118 (**sec. 155**).

Other exceptional idioms are of two kinds. (1) After **dic, doce, rogo vos** etc., the question is really direct and the indicative may be used: as, **dic, quaeso, num illa te terrent?** Cic. *Tusc.* i 5 10: **193.** (2) After **aspice ut, viden' ut,** the indicative is often found: either for the above reason or because the idea of question is lost in that of exclamation, or, like δηλονότι, the **aspice ut** etc., becomes an adverb. **Nonne vides, croceos ut Tmolus odores, India mittit ebur** Virg. *Geo.* i 56: **Aspice ut insignis spoliis Marcellus opimis Ingreditur** *Aen.* vi 856: **laetantur ut omnia** *Ec.* 4 52: **viden' ut geminae stant (? stent) vertice cristae** *Aen.* vi 779. Such expressions as **mirum quantum** and **nescio quis** are in effect single words. **Forsitan** properly requires the Conjunctive Mood, but late writers use it with the Indicative only. **Nescio an** *I rather think*, but in late Latin, *I don't know whether* Plin. *Ep.* vii 19 **sec. 153.** The latter by **-ne** in Cic. *Fam.* ii 5 2.

A question repeated in surprise by the person addressed is put in the Conjunctive. **Quid narras? Ego quid narrem?** Ter. *Phorm.* iv 4 4. A question in the plup. conj. asked indirectly is changed into the future participle or gerundive with **fuerit, fuisset,** or the infinitive with **possum** or **debeo.** The **sequence of tenses** is observed. **Quîn** consecutive keeps the primary sequence. See further **sec. 206, 223.**

Indirect **deliberative** question **Unde vitam sumeret inscius** Hor. *Od.* iii 5 37.

181. The verb in the Conjunctive is omitted only in late Latin. **Quis ille flebilis sonus?** Tac. *Ann.* i 41 above.

Person in Indirect Question. Real questions are in the

Conjunctive whatever the person. Those in the Second Person are, as a rule, real questions, since a man is more likely to know about himself. But a rhetorical question is always in the Infinitive, even in the Second Person: **quid eos** (*you*) **per populum egisse?** Liv. iii 39 9: **quid se vivere?** vii 18 5. So impersonally **quid enim ultrà differri** xxi 53 3. But not if an answer is possible, though it be in the Third Person. **Qui si improbasset, cur ferri passus esset?** Caes. *b. c.* i 32 3 (Riemann). A real question (not an exclamation) occurs in the Infinitive in Cic. *Ep. ad Brut.* ii 5 4: **quum quanto meum filium in periculo futurum diceret.**

182. Four persons or groups are concerned in Oratio Obliqua. *I*, the reporter or historian. *You*, his audience or reader. The original speaker and his audience. The last two must be generally included in the Third Person; the former (generally) distinguished by **se,** which however may, in its ordinary reflexive meaning, refer to his audience or again to a person spoken of. For the reflexive use see under Pronouns **sec. 87.**

Ipse may be used as well as **se** for the speaker or his audience or persons spoken of; its use is to distinguish either by emphasis or by gender and number. **Is** occasionally (**87**).

Some Relative and Interrogative Clauses in Indirect Speech.

Non habeo governs either the Deliberative Question (Greek Conjunctive) or Final Conjunctive (Greek Future). Cicero therefore has either **non habebam quid scriberem** or **nihil habebam quod scriberem** (besides **habui dicere** *N. D.* iii 39 93). In positive sentences only the relative is used. **Cur** may be interrogative or relative: the former in **cur sit lata [lex] ipsum indicabit tempus** Liv. xxxiv 6 10. So with **quare. Quid fuit causae** is followed either by **cur** or **quod,** both relative. **Quid fuit causae cur in Africam Caesarem non sequerere?** Cic. *Ph.* ii 29 71.

Vivid Construction, sec. 120—122. **Clauses subordinate to Indirect Speech** and **Virtual Indirect Speech**, sec. 119—122, 192—193.

RELATIVE CLAUSE

183. When the Relative Clause contains another clause depending on it, the relative frequently takes its construction from the dependent clause; as, **nec Alpes aliae sunt, quas dum superant, comparari nova possint praesidia** Liv. xxi 14 15: **cui male si palpere recalcitrat** Hor. *S.* ii 1 20.

The **Co-ordinate Relative** and its adverbs introduce new and independent matter, as, **qui** *and he*, **quanquam, etsi** *and yet*, **quum quidem** and 'inverse' **quum.** The neuter **quod** especially is used with **si, nisi, quia** etc., or alone: in the last case to be distinguished from **quod** causal and substantival.

The Co-ordinate Relative may express a passionate transition. **Quod te per caeli iucundum lumen...oro** Virg. *Aen.* vi 363: **quos ego**—without a verb i 135: **at Trebonio persuasi: cui ne suadere quidem ausus essem** Cic. *Ph.* ii 11 27: **en dextra fidesque, Quem secum patrios aiunt portare penates** Virg. *Aen.* iv 598: **quibus haec medii fiducia valli...Dant animos** ix 142. (So **Vel quum** in xi 406.) Cicero uses it commonly in apropos digressions.

Co-ordinate Relatives in Oratio Obliqua take the Infinitive Mood. **Ex quo illud naturâ consequi** Cic. *Fin.* iii 19 64: **aram esse, cuius cinerem nullo moveri vento** Liv. xxiv 3 7 may come under this head: add **quos omnes habendos hostes** viii 29 4: so **quum interim plebem obiectari aliis atque aliis hostibus** vi 27 6; see **sec. 135** for a different infinitive.

In parenthesis the co-ordinate relative may express **a wish**: as in the common phrases **quod bene vortat: quod bonum felix faustumque sit.**

184. The Defining Relative (co-ordinate or subordinate). The defining relative when repeated in another case may be exchanged for **is** etc., as in Lucr. i 21—22 **quae quoniam...gubernas, nec sine te quidquam...exoritur** (sec. 90 further).

An important case is that of the Universal Relative, which, except in late Latin, invariably takes the indicative, expressing Class concretely. **Felix qui potuit** Virg. *Geo.* ii 490: **quo nos cumque feret** Hor. *Od.* i 7 25: **omne tulit punctum qui miscuit** *A. P.* 343. Even **quum** takes the indicative, meaning *whenever.* The sense of frequency is not expressed: the perfect (or pluperfect) common in these cases expresses previous action. **Si quando in tergum pulsa recessit Dirigit** Virg. *Aen.* xi 653: **quotiescumque me viderit** (fut. perf.) **ingemescet** Cic. *pro Sest.* 69 146. Both verbs may be in the same tense; aorist **quum opus fuit adiuverunt** Liv. xxxiv 5 10: perfect **quoscumque audivi placavi** Cic. *Q. f.* i 2 2: perfect of custom **qui miscuit** above.

THE CONJUNCTIVE RELATIVE CLAUSE

(Qualifying Relative)

185. The Relative with the Conjunctive takes the place of a qualifying adjective, and with its antecedent forms an abstract noun of Class. As such it forms part of abstract expressions such as **fieri quod velit** the infinitive of **fit quod volo, felix sit qui nihil cupiat** (concretely **felix est qui nihil cupit**), and of Oratio Obliqua—**frumentum flagitat quod polliciti essent,** corn real only to the speaker and his audience. With indicative verbs the conjunctive **qui** clause makes a further statement qualifying the whole sentence.

186. With the verb 'to be' it signifies the existence of a class; as, **sunt qui non habeant** Hor. *Ep.* ii 2 183, the rest of the line **est qui non curat habere** referring to an individual, *i.e.* the poet. Taken as one word, **sunt qui** with the indicative may signify a great number, as **sunt quos...collegisse iuvat** Hor. *Od.* i 1 3.

Pauci sunt qui, inventi sunt qui, nemo or **quis est qui** with conjunctive are particular statements of an abstract class; *doers* (not *the doers*) were few or were found. **Quotus quisque erat qui rempublicam vidisset?** Tac. *Ann.* i 3, *How few there were who had known freedom?* **Solus es cuius in victoriâ ceciderit nemo nisi armatus** Cic. *pro Deiot.* 12 34. In **quidquam bonum est quod non eum qui id possidet meliorem facit?** the question is about a certain thing being good not about the class good (Cic. *Par.* i 3 14). The French *le plus brave qui vienne* has no real parallel in Latin except perhaps under **limiting qui** below.

187. The Conjunctive Relative Clause is used as an abstract object to **transitive verbs** as **mitto, creo, habeo: misit oratores qui pacem peterent.** Hence if a proper name is used, it is not the object but in defining apposition to it: as, **ea qui conficeret, Trebonium misit** Caes. *b. g.* vii 11: this is rare. This (**final**) use of **qui** differs from that of **ut** in implying the fulfilment of the purpose.

An impersonal form of the above is that of **final quo** (**quî** in Com.), signifying the measure of difference that one act is to make to another. Tacitus and Sallust use it without the regular comparative (**53**): **neque contra patriam neque quo pericula aliis faceremus** Sall. *Jug.* 33: **quo lamentatio minueretur** with implied comparative Cic. *de leg.* ii 26 65 [on the other hand **ut libentius faciatis** *pro Arch.* 11 28]: **ego id agam quî ne detur** Ter. *And.* ii 1 35 and **ut quî** (consequence) Plaut. *Capt.* 550: causal **quippe quî** (indic.) *Aul.* 349: with a **wish** *Men.* 451. **Non quo** *not that, not because* is used without any comparative.

As an **abstract complement** to a concrete noun this clause states a property of the subject. **Is est qui opes contemnat = contemptor est opum** and implies that such a one **contemnit opes.** In late Latin it is coupled to another adjective: **metuens virgae et cui non eliceret risum caudatus terga magister** Juv. vii 212: **iuvenes ipsius consulis et quos Magnum aliquid deceret** viii 262: **liberator Germaniae et qui imperium lacessiverit** Tac. *Ann.* ii 88.

188. Again, **like the adverbial adjective,** it qualifies a sentence by generalising one of its terms: **litteras quas me sibi misisse diceret recitavit** Cic. *Phil.* ii 4 7 (*a letter which*, not *the* letter): not Oratio Obliqua, which would be **misissem: rediit quod diceret** *Off.* i 13 40 is similar, meaning not *because he said*, but like the French *en annonçant.* **Quum e viatore esset auditum qui diceret** (*Att.* ix 11 1) might be due to **Modal Balance, sec. 228.** The qualification may itself be a particular fact; as, **qui ex ipso audissent nefaria quaedam ad me pertulerunt** *persons who had his authority informed me* Cic. *Att.* xi 8.

189. So in **Causal qui** (**ut qui, quippe qui**) the conjunctive clause qualifies the main sentence by quoting one of its terms as a **type. Ad Petelinum lucum, unde conspectus esset...concilium indictum** Liv. vi 20 11: **Pythius, qui esset gratiosus...convocavit** Cic. *Off.* iii 14 58 (*a popular man to be sure*). This is well seen when another reflection is added: **religione tactus hospes, qui omnia cuperet rite facta, descendit ad Tiberim** Liv. i 45 12. When the reason is given by **qui** with the Indicative, as in **di persolvant grates** [**tibi**] **qui Fecisti** Virg. *Aen.* ii 539, the verb to **qui** makes no new statement and the main verb is not qualified. So the parenthetical **quâ es prudentiâ, quae est tua prudentia** are not reflections qualifying the fact, but facts in illustration (comp. **ut est frequens municipium** Cic. *Ph.* ii 41 106). Sallust uses **quippe qui** with Indicative.

Another form of qualification is made by **Concessive qui,** which contrasts two contrary acts of the same person. **Qui chirographa Caesaris defendisset is leges Caesaris evertit** Cic. *Ph.* ii 42 109.

Preceded by an adjective the conjunctive **qui** qualifies it **like an adverb. Infelix qui non audierit** Virg. *Aen.* ii 345: **demens qui simularet** vi 590. With words of fitness it expresses the kind of fitness, as with **dignus, aptus,** and comparatives with **quam.**

190. Limiting qui qualifies by degree. When the conjunctive is used the writer seems to correct his whole statement by a new one: when the indicative, he is defining an inaccurate term. Thus perhaps naturally the indicative is used in limiting a request: **quod sine dolo malo facere poteris** Liv. xliii 15 8. The difference is often slight. Instances of conjunctive are **quod sciam, quod litteris exstet, quod inter auctores conveniat** vi 12 6: **quis qui paullum modo nosset...unquam protulit** Cic. *Phil.* ii 4 7: **Xenophanes unus, qui deos esse dicat, divinationem sustulit** *de Div.* i 3 5. Of the indicative, **quantum scio, qui quidem nunc sunt, ut hominem praestare oportet** Cic. *de imp.* 24 70. Limit is also expressed by consecutive **ut, ne** and conditional **dum**: sec. **209, 222.**

191. In later Latin abstract relative clauses become more frequent as language becomes more logical in form, *i.e.* more rhetorical. The change begins with the historic tenses; **quum** showing the tendency from the first. **Erat Athenis, si fraus capitalis non esset, quasi poenae aestimatio** Cic. *de Or.* i 54 232: **quum in convivium venisset** (*whenever*), **si aspexerat...abstinere non poterat** *ii Verr.* iv 22 48: **quoquo modo custoditus esset, effugere non poterat** *pro Cael.* 5 11: **erat, quum disputaretur, argumentorum copia** *Brut.* 38 143: **quum lustraret, eligebantur** *de Div.* i 45 102: **quibus opus esset, metum offerre solebat** *ii Verr.* ii 54 135: **mille et octoginta stadia quod abesset videbat** *Acad.* ii 25 81: **qui praestitisset...de eius famâ nemo loquebatur** *pro Cael.* 5 11: **prout postularet locus** Liv. v 47 2: **plerique necati si offendisset** ix 6 2: **dum gererentur** (*while*) x 18 1.

Tacitus, though not abandoning the old indicative use in generic clauses, carries the conjunctive further into primary tenses. **Ubi sanguis in artus se suffuderit, levi ictu cruorem eliciunt** *Ann.* xii 47: **tegumen sagulum fibulâ aut si desit spinâ consertum** *Germ.* 17. Late Latin also greatly extends the number of relative words thus used, including **quicumque, quotiens, nisi** (**nihil domi impudicum nisi dominationi expediret** *Ann.* xii 7), **ubi, ut, utcumque, ut quis, dum** and **donec** *while* and *until*, and many others.

192. The Qualifying Relative Clause **in indirect speech** (actual and **virtual**) with its antecedent forms a conception abstract to all except the speaker or person whose thoughts are quoted and his audience. Such a person is often needlessly introduced by commentators to explain the qualifying relative clause, as in the abstract **quod**-clause etc. Some striking instances of '**Virtual oratio obliqua**' are however: **nimium vobis Romana propago Visa potens, superi, propria haec si dona fuissent** Virg. *Aen.* vi 872: **minitans ni servaretur** Tac.: **nisi reddidisses minaci Voce dum terret** *unless you restore* Hor. *Od.* i 10 9: **(censorem) creavit ut qui optimo iure creatus esset** Liv. x 34 11. For the **tense** see **sec. 119—122.**

193. The mood of the subordinate clauses in Indirect Speech is indicative when the **words are those of the writer. Si moritur, probè factum videri** Liv. viii 10 12 after '*I ought to add*': **corpora (quae iacebant) redderet** Virg. *Aen.* xi 102: **scitote oppidum esse nullum ex iis oppidis in quibus consistere praetores solent...**, the rest of the sentence as in direct narrative Cic. *ii Verr.* v 11 28. More difficult if correct is **simul ad L. pugnatum audierunt, pro victis Romanos habuisse** Liv. ix 25 5: perhaps he is only giving the drift. In **dic hospes Spartae nos te hic vidisse iacentes dum ...obsequimur** Cic. *Tusc.* i 42 (quoting Simonides) the indirect form passes into the direct since the same person gives the message and the information.

SUBORDINATE CLAUSES WITH CONJUNCTIONS

194. Subordinate Clauses with conjunctions (Substantival or Adverbial: some have been mentioned already under the Qualifying Relative).

Quod Substantival Clause. This is really a Defining Relative Clause containing its own antecedent and therefore in effect a concrete substantive. It is not essentially different from **quod** Causal, but is entirely different from Co-ordinate **quod** *as to which*: **sec. 183.**

The **quod**-clause stands sometimes in apposition to a particular word. **Omitto illa vetera, quod istum...ille aluit** Cic. *Att.* viii 3 3: **pro eo quod** Liv. ix 8 15: **hinc...quod** Cic. *Q. F.* i 1 33: **quod Silius te loqui vult, potes id facere** *Att.* xii 30: **quod C. Pansa verba fecit, de ea re ita censeo** *Ph.* x 11 25. In the familiar **quod dicis, quod scribis,** it is in apposition to the sentence quoted (**196**).

195. The **quod**-clause is often used as the direct subject or object of the main sentence. **Occurrit quod** Caelius in Cic. *Fam.* viii 6: **gratulor quod** or with accusative and infinitive or an accusative of the fact. **Mitto quod** Plin. *Ep.* viii 6: **mirari se dicebat quod non rideret aruspex aruspicem quum vidisset** Cic. *de Div.* ii 24 51. More rarely **scio quod** Plaut. *Asin.* 51–2: **renuntiaverunt quod** *Bell. Hisp.* 36.

The **quod**-clause in the conjunctive does not necessarily imply indirect speech or thought. **Laudat Panaetium quod fuerit abstinens** Cic. *Off.* ii 22 75 *he praises Panaetius for moderation* in the abstract. So with **paullo post rediit quod se oblitum aliquid diceret,** *en annonçant,* not oratio obliqua; see **sec. 188.**

CAUSAL CLAUSE

196. The Conjunctive differs from the Indicative as abstract from concrete, not necessarily implying thought, as above. **Invisus Tiberio quod eum Rhodi agentem nullo officio coluisset** Tac. *Ann.* ii 42, *hated him as having failed in attention.*

Causal quod (like **quod** Substantival) is merely the neuter of the defining relative, both meaning *as to* a certain act: **cum tibi agam gratias quod me vivere coegisti** Cic. *Att.* iii 3. **Gaudeo quod** might belong to either. So it may denote any loose connexion: **Quod non Taenariis domus est mihi fulta columnis...At musae comites** Prop. iv 1 49: **quod te liberatum metu cogites** (conjunctive *as to your thinking*) **ornamenta ista minore negotio retinentur** Cic. *ii Verr.* v 68 175: **hoc erat...quod me eripis, ut** *this was the object of your* *saving me* Virg. *Aen.* ii 664: **esse quod reficerent** *there was a reason why* Liv. vi 39 11. **Quoniam** *whereas* is used in the same way: **quoniam discerni placet...nobiscum vero foedus est ictum** Liv. xxi 18 8.

Non quod, non quia and **non quîn.** In Lucretius and older Latin **non quod** is regularly used with the indicative (so **quiane auxilio iuvat ante levatos?** Virg. *Aen.* iv 538). **Rancidum aprum antiqui laudabant: non quia nasus Illis nullus erat** Hor. *Sat.* ii 2 90. The conjunctive came to be used when the reason denied was also false in fact. It really means *not that, i.e.* denies the connection with the supposed cause.

Non quo, for **non quod,** is used only with the conjunctive: as is also **non quîn.**

197. Quum Causal. This, really a temporal word, is often used with the conjunctive to qualify the main clause, not to relate a fact. In this sense it often follows the main clause. **Solitudinem [plebs] circa decemviros intueri: quum et ipsi interpretarentur** Liv. iii 38 10: **praesertim quum tot essent circa hastam illam qui alia omnia auderent** ironically *and that though* Cic. *Phil.* ii 26 64. **Quum** causal with indicative Plaut. *Capt.* 356.

198. Dum Causal. Dum, a temporal word, has a quasi-causal sense, when the end attained is the reverse of that aimed at, the opposite of **quum** which gives the logical cause. **Dum vitant stulti vitia in contraria currunt** Hor. *Sat.* i 2 24: **Vidi et crudeles dantem Salmonea poenas Dum flammas Iovis et sonitus imitatur Olympi** Virg. *Aen.* vi 585: **hi, dum aedificant tanquam beati, in aes alienum inciderunt** Cic. *ii Cat.* 9 20: **ita, dum pauca mancipia Agonis retinere vult, fortunas omnes libertatemque perdidit** *div. in Caec.* 17 56: **miles ignarus dum nautas intempestive iuvat officia prudentium corrumpebat** Tac. *Ann.* ii 23: **dum veritati consulitur, libertas corrumpebatur** i 75: **neque, dum procellas Cautus horrescis, nimium premendo Litus iniquum** Hor. *Od.* ii 10 2: **solus Dolabella Cornelius, dum anteire ceteris parat,**

absurdam in adulationem progressus Tac. *Ann.* iii 47: **dum adsident, dum deflent, saepe eodem rogo cremabantur** *ib.* xvi 13: **dum sidera servat, Exciderat** Virg. *Aen.* vi 338. This use is never conjunctive in Or. Obl.

Without **dum** the same effect is produced: **brevis esse laboro, Obscurus fio** Hor. *A. P.* 25.

The **tense** is Historic Present as with **dum** *while*: but the Primary Perfect is found. **In has clades incidimus dum metui quam cari esse et diligi maluimus** Cic. *Off.* ii 8 29. **Dum** (Aristo et Pyrrho) **in unâ virtute sita omnia esse voluerunt, virtutem ipsam sustulerunt** Cic. *de fin.* ii 13 43: **dum voluit...inventus est** *Brut.* 81 282. With pluperfect: **dum unam in partem oculos animosque hostium certamen averterat...capitur murus** Liv. xxxii 24 5. The perfect **avertit** would have been ambiguous.

199. Cause may be expressed parenthetically after the effect by **ita** and **adeo. Ita capta lepore** etc. Lucr. i 15: **adeo, quantum rerum minus, tanto minus cupiditatis erat** Liv. *praef.* 8.

A cause or concession may also be expressed by rel. with conj. or by an adj. with **homo** etc.: see under **Adjective (Adverbial use).**

TEMPORAL CLAUSE

200. Temporal Clauses are properly in the Indicative; and so **quum** *at the time when* = **quo tempore,** not relating but fixing the time of something else, takes the indicative, sometimes with **iam tum** *so early*: **etiam tum** *even from the time*: **quum dies venit** *at the time of the trial* Liv. vi 20 4: even with hist. pres. like **dum** *while*: **quum occiditur...fuerunt** Cic. *pro Rosc. Am.* 41 120. And of measured time **multi anni erant quum** Liv. ix 33 3 (**fuerant**).

Quum with present and imperfect indicative also expresses *identity or compatibility* between two acts. **Quum tacent clamant** *their silence cries aloud* Cic. *Cat.* i 8 21.

Inverse or Co-ordinate quum (*and then*) is a co-ordinate relative: its clause is practically the main statement, **sec. 183.** So **quum interea, quum interim** Liv. v 54 5 which also take the concessive conjunctive (**225**). **Quum** with hist. inf. **135**: with acc. and inf. **183**.

Narrative quum. Quum *when*, expressing an artificial connection between acts in the past, takes the conjunctive in narrative only. This idiom of regarding a past temporal connection as abstract or logical is peculiar to Latin. But compare with it the adverbial χθιζὸς ἔβην for χθὲς ἔβην (Lat. **hodiernus feci** for **hodiè feci 81**). Time easily merges into qualifying circumstance. When there is a real connection in logic we find **quum** sometimes following the main sentence: **illud egit quum demonstraret** *this he pleaded showing* (in later Latin **demonstrando**) Cic. *pro Sest.* 57 122.

For **quum** *whenever* see under **Relative Clause, 184, 191.**

Ut (1) *ever since* = **ex eo quum: ut abierunt hic tertius est annus** Pl. *Stich.* 29. (2) *as soon as*: **ut cessit, facili patuerunt cardine valvae** Juv. iv 63.

201. Postquam (simul simulac) 'now that,' semi-causal of a hindrance removed, takes all indicative tenses except the future. **Postquam citati non conveniebant** Liv. iii 38 12 *seeing they would not appear.* With aorist-perfect **postquam exempta fames** *when hunger was appeased*; and so commonly. Or of an interval: **postquam omnis res mea Ianum Ad medium fracta est, aliena negotia curo** Hor. *Sat.* ii 3 18: **undecimo die postquam in urbem venit** (or **post undecimum diem quam**). (With pres. ind. **104** *b.*)

Ante is often separated from **quam** for emphasis; as in Virg. *Ec.* 1 61 **ante leves ergo...quam...vultus**: regularly after a negative. **Antequam** and **priusquam** in Livy commonly take the conjunctive (*before such time as*).

202. Dum and **donec** 'while.' (**Donec** only in early and late Latin, the latter including Livy.) The conjunctive is used when there is more than mere coincidence. **Quattuor milia armatorum,**

dum recens terror esset, misit Liv. xxxvi 9 13: **illa quidem, dum te fugeret...non vidit** Virg. *Geo.* iv 457: **dum conderet urbem** *in the attempt to found*, *Aen.* i 5: **nihil sanè trepidabant, donec...agerentur** Liv. xxi 28 10. Once the present indicative is found with a purpose but rather inferred than expressed. **Tantum ibi moratus dum milites discurrunt** Liv. xxvii 42 13. Comedy of course always keeps the indicative. **Dum eximus opperibere** Ter. *Haut.* iv 7 5 (107). The imperfect and future tenses are in general used only with the meaning *as long as*: but in Liv. v 47 1 **dum agebantur...fuit** in the sense *while*. **Dum causal** is more elastic (**sec. 198**).

203. **Dum** 'until,' with **antequam** and **priusquam**, follows the same principle till Livy's time. **Antequam nox venit** *before night fell*: **antequam nox veniat** *before nightfall.* Livy generally uses the conjunctive and Tacitus always. **Corpus antequam cremaretur nudatum in foro** *Ann.* ii 73, as we say *awaiting burial.*

Donec, *until*, is rare in Cicero's time. It is used of facts by Livy and Tacitus with the conjunctive. **Trepidationis aliquantum edebant donec quietem timor fecisset** Liv. xxi 28 11: **donec praelium nox dirimeret** Tac. *H.* iv 35: **donec in Chattos usque sinuetur** *Germ.* 35: **petitione abstinuit donec ambiretur** *Ann.* ii 43. Cicero sometimes has **exspecto ut: exspectabant si nostri transirent** Caes. *b. g.* ii 9 1.

THE **UT**-CLAUSE (Substantival and Adverbial)

204. In the first case, which is only a simpler form of the other, the **ut**-clause is an abstract substantive. Properly the subject of impersonals, **integrum est ut** Cic. *pro Mur.* 4 8 (**eo decursum esse ut** Liv. xxii 31 10): **fuit ut** *pro Cael.* 22 48: and the common **fore ut, tantum abest ut, verisimile est ut** etc. Or in apposition to the main sentence, like the clause with **id quod** (**id quod supra memoravi**): **ut nihil sententiàe suae mutaret** Liv. ix 3 9: or in apposition to a noun: **foedus dictum ut in dicione essent** ix 20 8. As an exclamation: **te ut ulla res frangat!** Cic. *Cat.* i 9 22.

It has many substantival uses as object, which cannot altogether be distinguished from the consecutive and final uses. **Furta paro belli ut obsidam milite fauces** Virg. *Aen.* xi 515: **eo decursum est ut** Liv. xxxi 10 *they adopted the expedient of*: **id paremus atque agamus ne Poeni maneant** xxvi 41. Of moral effect: **neque committam ut, dum vereare tu ne sis ineptus, me esse iudices** Cic. *de Or.* ii 4 16 (of foolish, careless or criminal actions): **mihi certum est non committere ut in hâc causâ praetor nobis consiliumque mutetur** *i Verr.* 17 53. **Facio ut** throws emphasis on a qualifying expression. **Fecit animo libentissimo ut ne de honore deiicerer** *i Verr.* 9 25: **sive enim illud irato ac percito animo fecisset ut incensus odio trucidaret inimicum** *was betrayed by anger and excitement into*, *pro Mil.* 23 63: **faciam hoc non novum, ut testibus utar statim** *i Verr.* 17 55. Or without emphasis, to balance: **hoc etiam faciunt, ut dicant** *this too men love to say* Lucr. iii 925: **plebem se fecisse ait, ut tribus patrimoniis deleniret** Cic. *pro Mil.* 35 95.

205. **Exspecto ut** is common as well as **dum** (Cic. *pro Rosc. Am.* 29 82): **spem adferunt ut** Cic. *de Am.* xix 68: **vincere ut** *prove that*, *force it to be so*, properly **vincere ut videatur** *force it to appear so*: **nec vincet ratio, tantundem ut peccet idemque** Hor. *Sat.* i 3 115. So **efficio 206**. **Vincere** is also used with accusative and infinitive.

Quam ut may balance or replace an ordinary accusative and infinitive: **citius dixerim iactasse se aliquos...quam ut quisquam vellet** Cic. *Phil.* ii 11 25: **quid tam incredibile quam ut...triumpharet?** *de Imp.* 21 62: or it may be the object of a sentence: **omnia passuros potius quam ut** Liv. ix 14 7, or subject 16: or without **ut**, as in Sall. *Jug.* 105 3.

Tantum abest is used with two **ut** clauses, the former substantival, the subject of **abest**, the latter consecutive. **Haud multum abest quîn** Liv. xlii 44 2 (**210**).

CONSECUTIVE CLAUSE

206. The Consecutive Clause is always in the Conjunctive in Latin, even of facts: differing in this respect from Greek, English, and French. *Tant il était insouciant qu'il tomba*, or *il était insouciant au point de tomber*: *ὥστε ἔπεσεν, ὥστε πεσεῖν that he fell*, *as to fall.* The importance of the connection in Latin overrides the importance of the fact. In Latin the nearest approach to the Fact Consequence is the 'Vivid' Perfect Conjunctive in Historic Time, marking an abstract act without time as distinguished from the imperfect of unreal state. **Milo hoc fato natus est ut ne se quidem servare potuerit quîn una rempublicam vosque servaret** Cic. *pro Mil.* xi 30: **in tantâ paupertate decessit ut quî efferretur vix reliquerit** Nep. *Arist.* 3: **ut quî** for **ut** in another sense in Comedy: **ain' eum morbum esse, ut quî opus sit** Plaut. *Capt.* 550. The **periphrastic forms** as **doliturus, dolendus fuerit, servari potuerit, debuerit,** never change to pluperfect in historic time after **ut** consecutive (nor after **non quîn, non dubium quîn,** which also emphasize **fact**). **Ut, si effugium patuisset, impleturae urbem tumultu fuerint** Liv. xxiv 26 12: **non quîn breviter reddi responsum potuerit, sed ut in perpetuum mentio finiretur** Liv. ii 15 2: **nec dubium erat quin... terga daturi hostes fuerint** iv 38 2. In **Indirect Question** the sequence is kept, **sec. 223.**

A consequence **including** a **purpose** is negatived by **ne** or **ut ne. Efficitur non ut voluptas ne sit voluptas** (as some wish) **sed ut non sit summum bonum** Cic. *de fin.* ii 8 24: so with **adsequor** etc. With **facio** Tac. *Agr.* 6 **fecit ne...sensisset (212).**

To the ordinary words balancing **ut**-Consecutive (**tam, adeo, ita** etc.) add **ille** and its adverbs: **illuc decidit ut. Ille erat ut odisset accusatorem suum** Cic. *pro Mil.* 13 35.

207. Consecutive ut is also used to **explain** the main sentence. **Sic interpretor sensisse maiores ut censuerint** Cic. *Phil.* ix 1 3: **haec quoque opportunitas...ut adsit, ut habeat exercitum**

de Imp. 17 50. These with **eâ lege ut, accidit ut, extremum fuit ut, reliquum est ut, exspecto ut** (above) are hardly to be distinguished from **ut**-substantival. So **duae res agendae sunt, ut et veterem tollatis** Liv. xxiii 3 5: **utne tegam spurco Damae latus?** Hor. *Sat.* ii 5 18 *What? hob-nob with servants?*

208. Tanti ut followed by the cost or sacrifice means *at the price of*, not *so valuable that*. **Quae tanti gravitas ut se tibi semper Imputet?** Juv. vi 178: **quae praeclara et prospera tanti Ut rebus laetis par sit mensura malorum?** (*worth having if*) x 97: **tanti tibi non sit opaci Omnis arena Tagi...Ut somno careas** iii 54. But **arbitrabatur tanti mortem esse P. Clodii ut** (*such a blessing that*) **aequo animo patriâ careret** Cic. *pro Mil.* 23 63. So Ovid *Her.* vii 71 and often. In Mart. viii 69 **tanti Non est, ut placeam tibi, perire, ut** follows **perire** (Duff).

209. Ut limiting. Very commonly **ut** limits the main sentence. **Ita laudo ut non pertimescam** Cic. *div. in Caec.* 13 44: **ita eras Lupercus ut te consulem esse meminisse deberes** *Phil.* ii 34 85. Independently: **at satis ut contemplata sis** Ter. *Haut.* iv 1 4. With negative **ut** becomes (1) **ut ne: ita utile ut ne planè inludamur** Cic. *pro Rosc. Am.* 20 55: **danda opera est ut etiam singulis consulatur, ita ut ea res aut prosit aut certe ne obsit** *Off.* ii 21 72: **ita se rem augere debere ut ne quid deperderet** *ii Verr.* ii 30 73: (2) **ne: exercitus in Siciliam relegatus est ne ante P. belli finem reportaretur** (archaic) Liv. xxv 5 11. **Ut ita dicam** (substantival or limiting) becomes **ne dicam: inconsiderati fuit ne dicam audacis** Cic. *Ph.* iii 5 12: but **ut nihil dicam de iis qui condemnarunt** *Clu.* 47 131.

A limit is equally expressed by **modo** and **dum** (**222**): **dum ut** *Att.* vii 23 3: or by **qui** limiting (**sec. 190**).

210. Quîn (quî non) Substantival or Consecutive. In every sense it must follow a negative or its equivalent: even a word of preventing requires a negative, to be followed by **quîn**. The original meaning is interrogative. **Non quîn** and **non dubium quîn** lay stress on **fact** and are used with the Vivid Sequence in the Perfect Conjunctive.

211. Preventing sometimes takes the Infinitive (**prohibiti praeripere** Tac. *Ann.* xiii 28), as well as **quominus** and **ne. Quum domino succurrere prohiberentur** Cic. *pro Mil.* 10 29. Similarly **deterreo ne** or **quominus;** but **agere quae ad iudicium pertinebant liberè comitiorum metu deterrebar** (with inf. for emphasis) *i Verr.* 9 24. Tacitus has **praepeditus premere** *Ann.* ii 73. With pluperfect conj. see **Final Clause.**

FINAL CLAUSE

212. The balancing words **eo, ideo, propterea, idcirco** etc., are the same for purpose and cause: **eo consilio** is final only.

Ut may be accompanied by **ne** when there is a positive besides the negative purpose: as, **ut ne confirmatio modum solum habeat, verum...** Cic. *de Inv.* i 29 45. Oftener in comedy: **ulciscar ut ne plane inluseris** Ter. *Eun.* iv 4 20: in letters: **ut ne quid salvis auspiciis agi posset** Cic. *Fam.* i 4 2: but not after Cicero. Practically positive in **Ei velim scribas ut nullam rem tam parvam putet quae parum me digna videatur** *Fam.* v 11 2. Comp. **sec. 209.**

The Perfect and Pluperfect Conjunctive are sometimes used in a final and semi-final sense, mostly with a negative to represent the future perfect indicative (*lest it might be found*). **Ne frustrà hanc spem conceperitis** Liv. xliv 22 4: **neve hoc impunè fuisset** Ov. *Met.* iv 798: **ne quid inausum fuisset** Virg. *Aen.* viii 205: **dum vela darent, si forte dedissent** *in hope that* ii 136: **ut aliqua in vitâ formido esset posita** Cic. *Cat.* iv 4 8. So in consecutive clauses denoting result of effort: **ne committeret ut frustrà properasset** Cic. *Att.* xiii 45: **ne cuius sacrilegium respublica sensisset** Tac. *Agr.* 6.

Sometimes **ut** is omitted. **Praemittit Achaten Ascanio ferat haec** Virg. *Aen.* i 644.

Ne dicam, nedum and **ne** *much less*, properly follow a negative. **Nihil istorum ne iuvenem quidem movit ne nunc senem** Cic. *Fam.* ix 26. Whether a verb follows **nedum** is indifferent. Livy is the first to use **nedum ut,** and the first to use **nedum** without a preceding negative: **vel socios nedum hostes** xlv 29 2: **novam (potestatem) eripuere, ne nunc ferant desiderium** iii 52 9.

CONDITIONAL CLAUSE

213. Properly the two moods are identical. **Si conabitur, silebit: si expilet, agat** Cic. *Off.* iii 23 90.

Both moods Indicative. The condition is relative to present time, but there is complete freedom as to tenses. **Si heri errasti cras te paenitebit: si potui, potero** Virg. *Aen.* iv 419. **Si quidem** (εἴπερ) is virtually causal: *since as a fact.* **Si luxerit** *as soon as it dawns* Martial iv 86 9. *If he comes* (ἐὰν ἔλθῃ) is future indicative in Latin. **Nisi forte,** ironical, is often followed by **quasi vero** or **proinde quasi. Nisi forte, quia perfecta res non est, non fuit punienda: proinde quasi exitus rerum non hominum consilia legibus vindicentur** Cic. *pro Mil.* 7 19: **nisi tamen** *not but that* Sall. *Jug.* 24 5.

Note the use with the present of anticipation (**present tense,** 107): **sic ignovisse putato si cenas hodie mecum** Hor. *Ep.* i 7 70: **si manet, si discedit** of future time: **si paret** legal formula. **Pergratum feceris si** Cic. *de Am.* 4 16, **sec. 118.**

214. Both Moods Conjunctive. The condition is either **unreal** or **abstract**: in the former the imperfect and pluperfect are used. (The distinction of imperfect and pluperfect is not one of time, as usual in English, but between general and particular, the latter including all acts present and past. (*a*) In the *if*-clause: **libera mortua essem nisi filium haberem** (εἰ μὴ εἶχον) Liv. ii 40 8: but **si mens non laeva fuisset** *had I not been misguided on that occasion* Virg. *Aen.* ii 56. (*b*) In the main sentence: **gauderem si accidisset**

I should have been glad if Cic. *Att.* viii 6: with **res in difficili loco fuisset** *there would have been a difficulty in that case*, *Fam.* xii 28.)

The Present Conjunctive is abstract without necessarily implying unreality. **Me dies deficiat si nunc vociferari velim** Cic. *ii Verr.* ii 21 52: **si negem mentiar** *de Am.* iii 10: **erubescant profecto si quis eis hoc obiciat** Liv. v 6 5: **si primâ repetens ab origine pergam, Ante diem componat Vesper** Virg. *Aen.* i 372: **ni mea cura resistat, Iam flammae tulerint** ii 599. But it is comparatively rare. It may of course refer to an unreal condition, but the unreality is not expressed. **Ni faciat...ferant** i 58. Compare **Sicilia tota si unâ voce loqueretur hoc diceret** (Cic. *div. in Caec.* 5 19) with **si tecum ut dixi patria loquatur nonne impetrare debeat?** Cic. *Cat.* i 8 19. Or even to an act unfulfilled: **spatia et si plura supersint Transeat** Virg. *Aen.* v 324: **ni docta comes Admoneat... Irruat** vi 292: **ineant pugnas, ni Phoebus noctem reducat** xi 912.

The **imperfect** is used of an unreal state whether conceived as present or as past, the **pluperfect** of an unreal act only, not necessarily in the past. Sometimes the tense of state is put for that of act in a 'vivid' sense: **quin protinus omnia Perlegerent oculis, ni iam praemissus Achates Adforet** *Aen.* vi 34: **Partem opere in tanto, sineret dolor, Icare, haberes** *ib.* 31. (See for this tendency under **Historic Present** and after **Sequence of Tenses, 104–5, 121–2.**)

215. The Perfect Conjunctive is used of an abstract condition (or concession) viewed generally **apart from time. Ciceroni nemo ducentos Nunc dederit nummos, nisi fulserit** Juv. vii 140. For instances with sense of time see under **Permissive Conjunctive, 127.**

The Present or Perfect can never be joined with the imperfect or pluperfect in a Conjunctive condition. Either both are considered abstract or both unreal.

216. The Second Person Singular with general meaning (*you* for *any one*) may be followed by an Indicative. **Decedunt si**

iacteris Lucr. ii 36: **cum videas effugiunt** *ib.* 41: **quocumque aspicias** Ov. quoted **sec. 89.** More instances are given under the **Conjunctive Mood, 130.** Perhaps refer here **si palpere, recalcitrat** Hor. *S.* ii 1 20 (**218** *c*).

217. The following are exceptions to the correspondence of Moods.

(1) **Indicative Condition with a Will-Conjunctive** in the Apodosis. **Moriar si vera non loquor** (*i.e.* **volo mori**): **peream si non optimum erat** Hor. *S.* ii 1 6, where **erat** is virtually Conjunctive. (So **ita vivam ut verè loquor** or without **ut.**) **Quam vellem Romae esses, si forte non es** Cic. *Att.* v 18. So in past time **si meis incommodis laetabantur, urbis tamen periculo commoverentur** (*ought to have been*) Cic. *pro Sest.* 24 54.

218. (2) **Indicative with Conjunctive Condition,** where an abstract condition either (*a*) strengthens, (*b*) qualifies a *fact* or (*c*) makes no real difference to it.

(*a*) **Etiam si taceant satis dicunt** Cic. *in Caec.* 6 21: so **nec me vis ulla volentem Avertet, non, si tellurem effundat** Virg. *Aen.* xii 204: **Si fractus illabatur orbis Impavidum ferient ruinae** Hor. *Od.* iii 3 8.

(*b*) **Numeros memini—si verba tenerem** (*and I only wish*): **Suaves res, si non et causas narraret** Hor. *S.* ii 8 92: **capax imperii—nisi imperasset** Tac. *H.* i 49: **multa putabant Ni** Virg. *Aen.* viii 522; or see (*d*) below: **deserit ni subeat** *Aen.* xii 732: **loquitur severe, si velis credere** Cic. *Att.* xiv 19 2: **si homines iuvare velint, sunt...** Liv. ix 23 10.

(*c*) **Si cupias, licebit** Cic. *ii Verr.* ii 69 167: **dies deficiet si velim** *Tusc.* v 35 102. Rare with him: but, **si quaeras, occidit** Ovid *H.* vii 83: **si curet, narrabo** Hor. *A. P.* 464—his favourite idiom: **si in Italiâ consistat, erimus una** (*in case*) Cic. *Att.* vii 10.

The instances in the second person singular given at the end of the Unreal Condition are only apparent exceptions.

219. (*d*) **With melius fuit, oportuit** etc., *it really was better or more fitting*: **nonne fuit satius?** Virg. *Ec.* 2 14. **Si sana mens fuisset, difficile fuit** Liv. ix 9 12: **fuit bellandum** = **fuisset** ix 7 7: **si faciant, poterunt** Lucr. i 655. The indicative expresses the fact of the fitness or possibility, and is thus both an indicative and a conjunctive. (**Optimum erat** and **poteras** have a further explanation: see the next paragraph.) **Si perfugisset, haud multum afuit quin** Liv. xlii 44 2: **quod si putasset, certè optabilius fuit Miloni dare iugulum** Cic. *pro Mil.* 11 31: so **agitasse constat...ni frustrà fuissent** Tac. *Agr.* 13. The peculiar **nec veni, nisi fata locum sedemque dedissent** Virg. *Aen.* xi 112, seems to mean *I am not here without the passport of fate.* **Venissem** would mean *I should not have come*, **venerim** *I should not come in any case.* Further under **Perfect Tense** (*a*) **112**.

220. (*e*) **Trudebantur in paludem nisi Caesar legiones instruxisset** Tac. *Ann.* i 63 is an extension of the meaning of **incompleteness** in the imperfect (and pluperfect, **109, 115**) seen especially in **poteras, fuerat melius.** These two tenses seem in themselves to have a semi-modal sense of unreality like that of the augmented tenses in Greek. **Effigies Pisonis in Gemonias traxerant ac divellebant ni** *Ann.* iii 14: **Sustulerat, nisi Faunus ictum Dextrâ levasset** Hor. *Od.* ii 17 29: **fames quam pestilentia tristior erat, ni annonae foret subventum** Liv. iv 52 4: so **hoc roboris erat** = **fuisset** ix 19 5.

The following are Virtual Oratio Obliqua: **nimium vobis Romana propago Visa potens, superi, propria haec si dona fuissent** Virg. *Aen.* vi 872: **minitans ni servaretur** Tac. *H.* i 75: **nisi reddidisses Voce dum terret...Risit Apollo** Hor. *Od.* i 10 12.

(3) **Conjunctive condition suppressed. Quid domini faciant, audent cum talia fures?** Virg. *Ec.* 3 16: **non ausim** *ib.* 3 32: **quid si idem certet** 5 9: **si forte** *in case* 6 57: **si ex habitu non ingenio spectetur** Liv. ix 18 2.

221. Conditions (or Concessions) may also be conveyed

(*a*) **by qui and its derivatives,** following the same rules as **si. Qui videret equum Troianum, urbem captam diceret** Cic. *ii Verr.* iv 23 52. The balance of moods in condition is strictly kept: **haec qui videat nonne cogatur?** Cic. *N. D.* ii 4 12: **qui vendat debeatne?** *Off.* iii 23 91: **Serviet aeternum qui parvo nesciet uti** Hor. *Ep.* i 10 41.

(*b*) **by an Imperative. Expende Hannibalem: quot libras in duce summo Invenies?** Juv. x 147: **Pone Tigellinum: taedâ lucebis in illâ** i 155: **dic...et eris mihi magnus Apollo** Virg. *Ec.* 3 104: **tolle hanc opinionem: sustuleris vitae societatem** Cic. *Tusc.* i 13 30: **quis me, fac velle, sinet?** Virg. *Aen.* iv 540.

(*c*) **by a statement or question,** in this case practically the same. **Laudis amore tumes: sunt certa piacula** Hor. *Ep.* i 1 36: **negat quis: nego** Ter.: **poscit; dandum est: rides; concutitur** Juv. iii 100: **negaro: videbor** Cic. *Phil.* xi 8 19: **in caelum, iusseris, ibit** Juv. iii 78: **Vultis et his mecum pariter considere regnis? Urbem quam statuo vestra est** Virg. *Aen.* i 572.

(*d*) **by the Conditional or Concessive Conjunctive** without Conjunction. **Dixerit hoc Epicurus: non magis pugnem** Cic. *Fin.* v 27 80 (**126**). **Fuisset** and **dedisses** under **Permissive Conjunctive, 127.**

(*e*) **by a Participle: vita me manens conficeret, dimissa liberaret** Cic. *Ph.* ii 15 37. Compare **sec. 146,** par. 3.

(*f*) With apodosis absent or incomplete: **minaci Voce terret nisi reddidisses** Hor. *Od.* i 10 9: **inimice lamnae nisi splendeat** ii 2 3 (**sec. 220**).

222. Dum, *provided that,* is mental, though temporal in form. **Est mihi tanti huius invidiae tempestatem subire dum...periculum depellatur** Cic. *Cat.* ii 7 15. *With* **ne,** or **ne** alone: **at enim ne quid** *de Imp.* 20 60. Less commonly **dum non: dummodo non pereat** Juv. vii 225: **dum ego non imiter tribunos** Liv. iii 21 6. Without conjunction: **velis tantummodo, expugnabis** Hor. *S.* i 9

54: **tantum reponas Sensibus haec imis** Virg. *Ec.* 3 54. **Dum ut** sec. 209. **Modo** is also used alone.

223. *Periphrastic apodosis.* For the conjunctive the future participle or gerundive of fitness may be used in any sentence with the indicative of **sum**, or in the passive the infinitive with **possum, debeo** etc. These indicatives again become conjunctives after **ut**-consecutive, **quîn,** and **quum,** and in Indirect Questions. For the tenses see below. Sometimes periphrasis is avoided by the 'unreal' pluperfect **cesserat** for **cessisset,** which again becomes **cessisset** after **ut: ut nisi foedus esset memoria cessisset** Liv. ii 33 9.

In Past Sequence **fuerit potuerit** etc. become **fuisset potuisset** in Indirect Question only (including **non dubius quîn**), but do not change after **ut** and **quîn** consecutive, as in **non dubium quîn** and **non quîn.** (**Consecutive Clause, 206.**)

CONCESSIVE CLAUSES

224. A concession is simply a magnified condition, and the forms are often the same. The indicative concession simply states the facts side by side: the conjunctive strengthens the main statement or affirms it more strongly: for the latter **ut sis tu similis Caeli Birrique latronum Non ego sim Capri neque Sulci** *I should not be any the more* Hor. *S.* i 4 69: **quam volent illi cedant otio consulentes tamen a P. R. revocabuntur** Cic. *Ph.* ii 44 113: so with **quamvis** *as you please*, **licet** *it is allowed*; **eas licet** *your going is allowed.* For the former **praestat: concedo** Quint. i 1.

Quanquam is used regularly with the indicative only, and **ut** and **quamvis** with the conjunctive: Tacitus uses **quanquam** for **quamvis: quanquam incipiat** *Germ.* 25: **quamvis** with indicative in Lucr. iii 403.

Si nescis *though you may not know* Virg. *Ec.* 3 23 is a form of concession.

225. **Quum** *although* (compare Fr. *tout en l'admirant*) takes the conjunctive and is usually balanced by **tamen.** Following the main sentence it may be accompanied by **tamen, interea, interim, praesertim** (*and that though*): so **ubi** *whereas* (**ubi, si acta res esset, non extarent** Liv. ix 5 4). In this position **quum interim** in Sallust and **quum tamen** in Lucr. are co-ordinate and take the indicative: **quum tamen** infin. in Indirect Speech Liv. vi 27 6. **Quanquam** and **etsi** are also used co-ordinately, as **quum** above. **Quanquam o! —sed** Virg. *Aen.* v 195. See further under the **Coordinate Relative, 183.**

Without a conjunction the conjunctive mood may be used alone, as in **luctere...proruet** etc. Hor. *Od.* iv 4 66 (**127**).

A concessive clause may also be expressed by **ut** and conj., **ut** ind. with **ita**, or by an adjective with **homo** etc. See under **Adjective, sec. 82.**

COMPARATIVE CLAUSES

226. Comparison of fact is in the Indicative; **aliter ac volui:** so commonly in similes. The same conjunctions **quasi** and **velut** are used by Lucretius for Fact and Thought. Abstract or Unreal Comparison is in the Conjunctive and qualifies as well as defines. **Quasi** and **tanquam** are both for **tam quam si** *just as if.* Observe the connection with the Conjunctive Condition: **laetius id accidit quam si referrent** Liv. iii 38 12. **Quasi verò,** contemptuous, is used by Cicero with the present and imperfect conjunctive: in the former case ironically considered as an abstract thought, in the latter as false. **Quasi** and **tanquam** are also used without a verb to qualify metaphor.

227. **Sicut** *as if* is late Latin. **Tanquam** and **quasi** lose their idea of falseness in Tacitus and Juvenal. **Iam Suspectus tanquam ipse suas accenderit aedes** Juv. iii 222: **increbrescente rumore tanquam commoraretur** Suet. *Tib.*; both of which accusations were probably true.

Comparative conjunctions are also used with participial clauses:

as, **velut posito bello** Liv. i 53 5: **haud secus quam pestifero sidere icti pavebant** viii 9: **tanquam non transituris in Asiam Romanis** xxxvi 41: **quasi praedâ sibi advectâ** Cic. *ii Verr.* v 25 64.

Ut comparative often means *considering* or *as was natural*: **ut in tali re** Liv. v 41 1, and **sec. 189.**

MODAL ATTRACTION AND BALANCE

228. When a verbal clause depends on a conjunctive it tends to be in the same mood; as in Greek a sentence governed by an optative tends to be in the optative also: *ὣς ἀπόλοιτο καὶ ἄλλος ὅ τις τοιαῦτά γε ῥέζοι.* **Tali memoriâ fuit, ut quae secum commentatus esset ea verbis eisdem redderet quibus cogitavisset** Cic. *de Or.* ii 1 1. Often indeed the subordinate clause may be considered at will either as defining or as qualifying: in the former case it is in the indicative, in the latter conjunctive. In rhetorical narrative the latter construction is preferred as giving unity to the period. **Quum eo Catulus et Lucullus nosque ipsi postridie venissemus quam apud Catulum fuissemus** Cic. *Acad.* ii 3 9: **accidit ut nonnulli milites qui discessissent interficerentur** Caes. *b. g.* v 39 2: **ut vestris etiam legionibus sanctus essem quod meminissent** (= **meminerant**) Cic. *Phil.* ii 24 60. On the other hand variety may be required by the sense: **nos isti hominum generi praecipue debere videmur, ut, quorum praeceptis sumus eruditi, apud eos quod ab eis didicerimus velimus expromere** Cic. *Q. f.* i 1 28.

229. A similar attraction is found in the use of the infinitive with **qui, quum, quam interim** etc., all of which may be used coordinately and take the construction of the main verb; as, **aram esse, cuius cinerem nullo moveri vento** (**Relative Clause, 183,** above).

SOME GRAMMATICAL FIGURES

230. The name **Hendiadys** may be given to a tendency of Latin not confined to poetry: it is due to the preference of noun and verb to adjective and adverb; arising again from the want of qualifying expressions already referred to **sec. 77.** As a rule one member of the figure qualifies or amplifies the other: *e.g.*, **partem et consuetudinem** *a habitual element*, Cic. *Fam.* iv 13 1: **usus et tractatio** (**dicendi**) *practical experience*, *de Or.* i 25 113: **magister atque artifex** *master of the craft* (*ib.*): **vim atque arma** *armed violence*, Liv. v 43 4: **fletum misericordiamque** *tearful appeal*, Cic. *de Or.* ii 45 189: **iudicium ac defensio** *defence at law* 48 199: **lepos quidam facetiaeque** *graceful wit* i 5 17: **luxum atque libidinem** *vicious indulgence*, Liv. *praef.* 9: **rationem naturamque** *essential principle*, Cic. *de Or.* i 18 80: **rem veritatemque** *actual truth*, *Tusc.* v 5 13: **voluntas studiumque** *earnest desire* 2 5: **pro iuventâ et errore filii** Tac. *Ann.* i 58: **navibus et casibus** xii 43: **tempore et spatio** ii 82: **urbe ac foro** *Hist.* ii 28. With verbs: **distinguere ac separare** *distinguish apart*, *ii Verr.* iv 41 88: **affari atque adpetere** *welcome with eagerness* and **expulsos et relegatos** *driven into banishment*, *Phil.* ii 13 33: **venditum et emancipatum** (**tribunatum**) *sold in open market*: etc.

Virgil's hendiadys would require a fuller space.

Asyndeton is a rhetorical expedient for contrast or dramatic effect; **sec. 113** (4), **198**, **221** end etc.: it is the *regular* construction in Cicero in phrases of more than two nouns naturally distinct, as **aetatum temporum civitatum** *de Or.* i 4 16.

Ellipse. Besides those mentioned in **secs. 90, 163**, the following are interesting: **Maecenas quomodo tecum?** Hor. *Sat.* i 9 42: **tam bonus gladiator rudem tam cito?** Cic. *Ph.* ii 29 74: **mecum uti voles** 46 118: **confestim ad eam** 31 77: **quo te, Moeri, pedes?** Virg. *Ec.* 9 1: **nisi reddidisses, minaci Voce terret** above **192**: **quid tu, inquit, huc?** Cic. *de Fin.* iii 2 8: **non ante datur...Quam qui** Virg. *Aen.* vi 141: **neu mortem in isdem laboribus** Tac. *Ann.* 1 35.

231. Hyperbaton: **Vina bonus quae deinde** Virg. *Aen.* i 195: **ludo fatigatumque somno** Hor. *Od.* iii 4 11 and often: **per te deos oro** and **per ego has lacrimas** Virg. *Aen.* iv 304: **idem pacis eras mediusque belli** Hor. *Od.* ii 19 28.

For **Constructio ad sensum** or **Synesis** see **secs. 4, 5, 6, 175**, and for **litotes** the expressions with **haud sec. 153**: add **nonnulli** *a few or many*, **95.**

Oxymoron: **Splendidè mendax** Hor. *Od.* iii 11 35: **insanientis sapientiae** i 34 2: perhaps **feros cultus** *barbarian civilisation*, i 10 2.

Zeugma: **moresque viris et moenia ponet** Virg. *Aen.* i 264: **iura magistratusque legunt** i 426 (*or* translate *ministers of justice* by hendiadys). Common in Sallust: **ubi aut quid agitaret** *Jug.* 54 2.

Chiasmus: commonly with **asyndeton**: **video meliora proboque: Deteriora sequor** Ov. *M.* vii 21: but **proelio strenuus et bonus consilio** Sall. *Jug.* 7 5.

Hypallage: see under **46, 77.**

For **attraction** see **secs. 228–9** above. The term is rather unsatisfactory, implying that there was an original 'regular' use. In early cases this is probably not true, as in the instances under **2, 7, 90.**

INDEX OF SUBJECTS

The Numbers refer to Sections

INDEX OF WORDS

The Numbers refer to Sections

INDEX OF AUTHORS QUOTED

The Numbers in heavy type *refer to Sections*

For EU product safety concerns, contact us at Calle de José Abascal, 56–1°, 28003 Madrid, Spain or eugpsr@cambridge.org.

www.ingramcontent.com/pod-product-compliance
Ingram Content Group UK Ltd.
Pitfield, Milton Keynes, MK11 3LW, UK
UKHW012332130625
459647UK00009B/242

* 9 7 8 1 3 1 6 6 1 1 9 6 8 *